Pain Free Living

THE EGOSCUE METHOD FOR STRENGTH, HARMONY, AND HAPPINESS

Pete Egoscue

with Roger Gittines, authors of *Pain Free*

STERLING ETHOS
New York

STERLING ETHOS
New York

An Imprint of Sterling Publishing
387 Park Avenue South
New York, NY 10016

ISBN 978-1-4027-8643-3

Distributed in Canada by Sterling Publishing
c/o Canadian Manda Group, 165 Dufferin Street
Toronto, Ontario, Canada M6K 3H6
Distributed in the United Kingdom by GMC Distribution Services
Castle Place, 166 High Street, Lewes, East Sussex, England BN7 1XU
Distributed in Australia by Capricorn Link (Australia) Pty. Ltd.
P.O. Box 704, Windsor, NSW 2756, Australia

For information about custom editions, special sales, and premium and corporate
purchases, please contact Sterling Special Sales at 800-805-5489 or specialsales@
sterlingpublishing.com.

Manufactured in the United States of America

2 4 6 8 10 9 7 5 3 1

www.sterlingpublishing.com

This book validates the wisdom, knowledge, and experience you have about your own
health. Because you know more about it than anyone else, I offer the following heart-
felt counsel: it's always a good idea to seek out and carefully listen to intelligent and
perceptive health-care advice. It's always a bad idea to act on that advice, including my
own, without fully accepting your paramount role in safeguarding the perfect health that
comes to us all as a precious human birthright and legacy.

CONTENTS

You Know: An Informal Introduction · iv

ONE · Good Cause · 1

TWO · The Calm · 15

THREE · Your Fuel Gauge · 29

FOUR · Fear and Limitation · 43

FIVE · Muscle Magic · 53

SIX · Balance of Forces · 61

SEVEN · Halo . . . Halo . . . · 67

EIGHT · Storytellers · 71

NINE · Blame Blam · 76

TEN · The Weight of Evidence · 84

ELEVEN · The Skeptic and the Gospel of Doubt · 98

TWELVE · Making the Worst of It · 115

THIRTEEN · Unstick This · 133

FOURTEEN · Wall to Wall, Y'all · 139

FIFTEEN · Conclusion · 156

Index · 158

Pain Free Living DVD Information · 165

About the Authors · 166

YOU KNOW:
An Informal Introduction

THIS BOOK IS A CELEBRATION. It is about the whole world—your world, your life.

It is about beliefs, actions, and consequences; about the truth concerning your deepest thoughts, where they come from, and what effect they have on your health and well-being.

Both the mutable facts of constant change and the immutable perceptions born of change fascinate me. Our home planet, a shimmering blue-and-green orb first seen in Apollo mission photos barely forty years ago, is a constantly changing place. Five centuries after Columbus boldly sailed west to reach the East (the first recorded case of *disorientation*, since he really only arrived in a backwater of the Western Hemisphere), the fundamental rounded shape of things seems to have been flattened by technology and relentless systemic upheaval.

The world continues to change. Humankind has evolved with a remarkable ability to change that has allowed us to survive, whereas most other life forms have not, and the majority of our earthly cohabitants are long gone. For some reason, the losers lost their innate ability to change: They depended on certain conditions— temperature, fresh water, sunlight, and the like. The ultimate survivalists are able to adjust the menu.

The human ability to change is linked with our internal monitoring systems. By paying attention to what the monitors perceive, we can alter our behavior.

I believe, however, that we are learning to ignore our internal mechanisms of perception to misuse important tools like our emotions, which have long protected us from surprise changes in the environment that are life threatening. Many of our monitors react automatically. For instance, they release immune cells to counter an infection long before a patient consciously notices a sore throat. Others depend on the individual to react by avoiding stressful behavior, taking a nap, or running away from a fight.

Medical science is attempting to cut those automatic links. We can't afford to let that happen.

The ancient Greeks imagined the life journey as traveling through a confusing labyrinth. I invite you to imagine with me that just around the next blind corner on a wall, inscribed in gold lettering, is an observation, inspired by spiritual teachings known as the Noble Eightfold Path of Buddhism: "Pain is inevitable; suffering is optional."

Who left the message? A seeker—someone just like you.

I intend to remind you of what it is that humankind has long sought and what you already know: truth dwells within; only awareness provides access to the enlightenment of ancient wisdom forged from experience. This book offers a renewal of that awareness, a renewal that leads to (and from) a powerful inner certainty about your health. Humankind possesses roughly a million years of practical, operational experience in dealing with pain. Yet starting comparatively recently, many of us have been beguiled by the idea that medical science knows so much about the inner workings of the body that this or that drug or surgical procedure—often with damaging side effects—offers the only real hope to those who are in pain.

It can be a comforting notion. Fortunately, though, when we try to command our bodies to shut up and butt out and get on with whatever breakthrough program is being presented to us by caring, dedicated, highly intelligent, and well-educated men and women working for our largest industry (health care), we can't help but notice the stirrings of deep misgivings. They are nothing less than beliefs that refuse to be betrayed, beliefs forged in the white heat of emotional experience and truth—a force inside that understands us more thoroughly than any other human being possibly could. Ignorance is a poor excuse for that particular form of bliss. We know: seeking to know is what we strive so long and hard to do. Despite what the experts tell us, our bodies, which are driven by hyper-vigilant sensory perceptions that I briefly touched on earlier, refuse to surrender a deep set of beliefs—perhaps life's most fundamental beliefs. Refusal is what this book is about, not the rejection of pessimism nor negation. This is a book of absolute optimism rooted in an amazing, bulletproof, nearly perfect belief system that functions in harmony with an equally amazing cellular/molecular-level command-and-control juggernaut.

Juggernaut? Probably an overstatement. Yet it is certainly a word that comes close to describing a mechanism that directs 60 trillion cells in a whirling, lifelong dance of unimaginable precision and complexity. In this case, the inaptly named juggernaut, partnered with the almost too familiar, too trite rubric of spiritual belief, is relying on that stubborn human trait (at the very least, obstinate doubt aimed at the notion that the body is frail and easily broken) to keep you skeptical and scrappy long enough to rediscover the healing power of inner truth.

Bravo! That's the good news. For a change there is no bad news; not from this quarter anyway. For nearly five decades I have had one simple paramount goal: help people who experience musculoskeletal pain recover their health without destroying the body's genius for recovering from accidents, illness, and aging and without surgical intervention or taking dangerous pain killers and other toxic drugs. We can do this. The book you are reading right now, as well as the DVD that's included, will serve as an easy-does-it guide and mentor. I started out in the 1970s making house calls.

That's right, house calls. Today the Egoscue Method has worldwide reach with twenty-four clinics in the United States, Europe, and Asia, along with a growing legion of independent alternative-care professionals I've been privileged to personally teach and certify.

Before we jump into Chapter One, I want to reveal an Egoscue Method secret: my techniques for non-medically dealing with musculoskeletal system pain are so effective because our most successful clients and readers come to us believing in the body's power to heal itself. We are all hardwired that way. Unfortunately for many people, things have gotten in the way of routinely accessing that belief. I'm going to use the book to bulldoze the obstructions. Have fun with the pages that follow, since having fun is usually a sign that we are doing the right thing. Glory in optimism. Then go for it—make a choice. Find lasting enjoyment; in every sense be *enjoyed. En riched.*

Remember—and rejoice that the memory persists within—that suffering is optional. You have the power to choose between sickness and health, hope and fear. Feel your way to the best of health.

Pete Egoscue

People say that what we're seeking is a meaning for life. I don't think that's what we're really seeking. . . . [W]hat we're seeking is an experience of being alive, so . . . that we have resonances within our innermost being and reality [and] . . . actually feel the rapture of being alive.

—Joseph Campbell

"Nothing can bring you peace but yourself."

—RALPH WALDO EMERSON

ONE

GOOD CAUSE

I KNOW A GUY WHO, FOR THIRTY YEARS—in the course of writing four books, taking part in more than a half-million clinical consultations, speaking at hundreds of seminars, giving media interviews, and conducting health workshops and classroom discussions—asked the wrong question over and over again.

Yeah, but the question sure did sound right:

"How do you feel?"

See what I mean? What could possibly be wrong about that? A lot. Now we know there was a trapdoor built into the sentence, hidden between the "do" and the "you." When the question was asked, the floor suddenly and silently dropped away, and a meaningful answer disappeared.

It's a fine, serviceable question—*How do you feel?* It seems to cover a lot of ground and leave enough space for "I feel cold," "I feel thirsty," "good," "bad," "better," or "worse." The question provokes a quick inventory of what's most bothersome, particularly pain—whether there is currently pain, or a fresh memory of it. If people happen to be pain-free when the question is asked, most tend to cautiously double-check in case it has managed to slip by them unnoticed. In the process, most other feelings—particularly those that can be transitory and fragile, such as happiness and peace of mind—are often overlooked.

Here's a more-or-less accurate translation of "How do you feel?" What's really being asked is "Do you feel pain? Where? Does it hurt more or less or not at all when you . . . ?" (Fill in the blank with one of a thousand possibilities.) Pain is pain for a reason: the official bearer of bad tidings, its duties include shouting down, distracting, and rudely jumping in line ahead of other feelings.

What this errant questioner should have been asking was, "What are you experiencing? Setting aside the pain for a moment if you can, please describe all the physical and emotional sensations that you perceive." Is it pain, or pain's sidekick—fear? Your body respects pain as an important messenger, but it deeply loathes fear. Among its other responses, the body reacts to fear by radically adjusting your internal chemical mix and modifying essential cellular functions, throwing some into hyper-drive and drastically curtailing others. The objective is to urgently fortify the membranes of your cells to exclude whatever it is that is giving off the smell, the taste, the vibes, the rot of fear and possible death.

This is a good thing, but damaging if pain is allowed to override all of the other feelings that often provide a more comprehensive and accurate reading of your health.

No Fooling

Pain is not an emotion, although it evokes strong secondary emotion-like states of mind. In the case of chronic, recurring illness, pain can lead to panic, dread, and depression, which are close cousins of fear. But first and foremost, pain is a symptom of a physical condition—a form of sensory perception that announces itself in a way that is impossible to ignore.

The mind has an amazing talent for converting routine physical sensations into conscious awareness that can instantly influence behavior without engaging in a formal, carefully executed cognitive process. Courtship and mating rituals are examples. Romeo and Juliet embraced first, and only later considered the pros and cons of love. Driven mad by jealousy deviously stirred up by Iago, Othello strangled Desdemona. Likewise, random mood swings seem to come and go independently of any obvious provocation. In a flash we jump from glad to sad, from selfish to generous, from calm to anxious. We slam down the phone, honk the car horn, or yell at the dog. Alternatively, perhaps we don't slam, honk, or yell—choosing instead to shrug or nod or smile. Some of us are better at managing our emotions. Managed well or poorly, the bottom line is that emotions convey messages inspired by direct interaction with the real world. Feelings allow us to re-experience the experience. Emotions tend to have an honest, utilitarian, and traceable lineage.

Fear instigated by pain, however, is a bastard that lacks the legitimacy of context. Once the sensory readout crosses the invisible threshold between mild and moderate discomfort, the response to pain isn't modulated by reason, recollection, or experience, like a relatively healthy emotion. Oh no. It hurts, and we want it to stop. The arc of escalation leaps from "so what?" to "I'm hurting...help!"

*   ★   ★   ★   ★

We are going to take a close look at why emotional escalation happens and what can be easily done to recover healthy control. For now, though, it is more useful to establish the powerful pain-fear connection, and introduce how it hijacks a fairly simple, orderly biomechanical sequence to set off a chain reaction of damaging consequences. By treating pain as just another emotional compo-nent that is always hovering nearby in moments of sickness and in health, Mr. How-Do-You-Feel unintentionally condemns those he is trying to help—except for a small minority—to the futility of symptomatic treatment, where pain escalates, despair and disorientation set in, and the body's amazing power to heal itself is compromised.

"My back hurts. . . ."

"My knee is killing me. . . ."

"These headaches are horrible. . . ."

What wonderful answers! Based on these responses, I could immediately go to work eliminating the pain. Except it was a symptom—perhaps not even the most important symptom—rather than the actual cause of very real, ultimately life-changing, and possibly life-threatening situations.

> If you break a leg in a fall, the fracture is the cause of pain, and the pain is obviously a symptom. But if a physician manages to kill the pain, the leg is still broken. Suppressing the pain symptom is relatively easy, but there is usually much more work to be done, and my point is that too often the work isn't done.

If you haven't guessed it by now, Mr. How-Do-You-Feel was me. I asked the wrong question again and again because I knew with absolute certainty that these painful conditions could be fixed with a few simple postural remedies. By asking, "How do you feel?" I really meant, "I already know. Save your breath. I can fix you." I had become an "expert," telling people what to do and how to do it. Meanwhile, I was criticizing other experts for offering remedies that substituted their knowledge and skills for the pain sufferer's own instincts. "The patient knows best," I insisted. "Each of us knows how we feel." The Egoscue Method—my life work—delivers results because it rests on trust that stems from how the patient really feels. Those feelings are always right.

I had only one problem: I didn't really believe it.

Don't worry, this book is about you, not me. I will get out of the way after presenting a bit more background. Then it will be my privilege to guide you on a journey of rediscovery that can change the way you experience the rest of your life. The Joseph Campbell quote before this chapter isn't just window dressing. It is the real deal—you *can* experience the rapture of being alive.

The Big Picture

Okay, back up three paragraphs to my first direct reference to the "Egoscue Method." As a non-medical postural therapy program, the Egoscue Method works, and works quickly. Often, in less than ten or fifteen minutes, there are dramatic results. Musculoskeletal system pain is accompanied by a distinctive posture. By changing the posture, the pain diminishes significantly or abates entirely. Typically, patients are evaluated by a therapist, coached through a customized series of postural exercises, and then they are sent home to do daily workouts for a week or two. When they return to us, we expect to see a big change. I never understood what was happening when I, or one of my staff therapists, asked "How do you feel right now?" as the second round of in-clinic treatment began. We'd hear the blandest of generalities come from 80 percent of our new patients. We would get "Fine," "So-so," and my least favorite, "I don't know, you tell me."

Huh? Run that by me again. So-so? You don't know . . . ?

Were these the same people who could barely move ten days before? Instead of high fives or rejoicing that the pain had subsided or gone away completely after weeks and even years of suffering, they had a forgetful, guarded, almost disbelieving attitude.

Often I had to press them to grudgingly admit, "Yes, my back feels much better." Or, "Pain comes and goes after I do the exercises you recommended instead of hurting constantly."

I'd glance at their original intake interviews and might note that the pain had caused severe insomnia. "How about sleep?"

"Oh, yeah, I'm sleeping better."

I dealt with these baffling responses by telling myself that these patients were so obsessed with their pain that they were unable to look beyond their symptoms and realize that by restoring their posture they felt a whole lot better in general. They had more energy, soaring activity levels, recovered mobility, improved mood, and so on. The vast macro changes didn't register on their consciousness, and the many significant micro effects of pain abatement seemed to be quickly forgotten or severely undervalued once the hurting subsided.

When I asked, "How do you feel?" I was focusing on the big picture, the *panorama* of benefits. Most people were satisfied if the pain *close-up* went way. They wanted a successful treatment, and that's what they got. Case closed. Move on. Many of them dropped out of the program (though overall, the percentage was single digit at worst), though they frequently returned eventually to seek our help later with other incidents of pain and dysfunction. I took this repeat business as a vote of confidence in the Egoscue Method.

Among those clients who stayed with the postural program, they reported feeling pain reduction and major improvements in energy levels, mood, balance, and sense of well-being. They didn't need prompting or prodding—they were excited and raring to do more. Frequently, it led to a total health makeover. Favorite sports and activities that had been put aside because of age or "wear and tear" were resumed and deeply savored.

The best I could explain it was that one group "got it" and the other didn't. I was right, but it took me a long time to figure out why.

★   ★   ★   ★   ★

The turning point was when I realized that even *I* didn't get it. I was treating my own body as if it were a machine: keep it fueled, lubricated, put air in the tires, and everything would be fine. I ran, lifted weights, took vitamins, and watched what I ate. After all, I was "the posture guy"; I worked conscientiously at tuning up my musculo-skeletal system, and pain was no longer an issue. Yet there were other issues: anger, frustration, regret, fear. On one level, I could say I felt okay. On another, I felt lousy. What was my body telling me?

Meanwhile, I was forced to grapple with an alarming business trend. Starting in the mid-1990s, my growing national network of Egoscue Method clinics was retaining a smaller and smaller percentage of the clients who started with us. Roughly eight to ten in-clinic therapy sessions of ninety minutes each would constitute "full" treatment. In most cases, full treatment meant a cure of the condition that brought the individual to us in the first place. In other words, our non-medical, postural therapy eliminated pain and physical limitation, and it restored musculoskeletal function. Less than 2 or 3 percent of our clients expressed dissatisfaction. Still, the fact that some weren't finishing the therapy cycle indicated there was a problem.

I ran the numbers over and over again in disbelief. Too many of my clients were dropping out of the program as soon as the pain abated, which in almost every case was before musculoskeletal system functions were fully restored. Our mantra was, and still is, "A cure, not just treatment." Why would patients settle for treatment when a comprehensive cure was available? I started quizzing those clients who remained. I wanted to know what was motivating them to continue.

Slowly, the pieces fit together. One, the Egoscue Method alleviated pain without surgery or drugs. Two, being pain free left the patient feeling healthier in general. And three, by escaping pain, regaining musculoskeletal alignment, and strengthening posture, those who persevered regained peace of mind and enormous self-confidence. Most importantly, what they felt sprang from their inner emotional perceptions, not from externally provoked physical sensations.

What I was looking at was a classic mind-body connection that confirmed my own personal experience. Often, troubling health issues are centered in the emotions rather than in any internal, physical malfunction or shortcoming. Since many of the major Eastern religions have led the way for centuries in exploring how and why the body and mind interact, it seemed reasonable to explore what those religions have learned. It has been an enlightening pathway, and I am grateful to the many helpful teachers, scholars, philosophers, and friends who have guided me.

This book sets out to demonstrate that the mind-body connection is the pivot-point on which your health balances. Furthermore, years of studying the human musculoskeletal system convince me that posture functions as an on-off switch that activates emotions. Through emotions, the musculoskeletal system allows you to optimize your health without the need for increasingly common, major medical intervention driven by experts, many of whom operate on the sincere but erroneous assumption that the body is fragile, makeshift, and prone to break down.

When the mind-body connection is working well, and working with fully balanced posture, you directly experience the effects of your external environment—an effusion of positive, pleasurable, life-affirming emotions that help regulate the mind and the body. Hence, cell membranes, which I already mentioned, do not need armor plating to exclude toxins. Nor is it necessary for the body to urgently adjust our inner chemistry by pouring hormones into the bloodstream or dumping T-cells into combat zones of infection like so many ninja warriors.

Balanced posture amounts to an unobstructed window. It tells us many things in real time about the landscape of our mind-body health, not the least of which is that positive energy is flowing in abundance through your cellular membranes—the "brain" of the cell. The destination for this energy is the mitochondria in each of the tens of billions of cells in your body. The mitochondria contain enzymes that accomplish electron transport, the citric acid cycle, and fatty acid oxidation to rejuvenate the cell with adenosine triphosphate (ATP), a concoction of oxygen, heat, water, and nutrients—the equivalent of jet fuel and matzo ball soup. The cells gorge on ATP, gobbling up and burning off the volume equivalent of half your body weight each day. Courage, calmness, strength, and renewal flourish. The cup runneth over, and it is on display in plain sight.

★　★　★　★　★

To survive, every form of life must stay in close contact with its external environment and engage in constant two-way negotiations. If the environment changes abruptly—and change is a historical certainty of living on Earth—the organism either adapts successfully to its new circumstances or dies. Of the 30 billion individual species of organisms believed to have existed on this planet since life first emerged, only a hundredth of 1 percent survives today. Extinction is the rule, not the exception. Clearly, change is not easy to accomplish. Contrary to popular belief, it is highly unlikely that the secret of our longevity is brain power—or to be more precise, "prefrontal cortex power." Cell power is probably more like it, cells being the classic know-it-alls. Each of your cells comes with a complete copy of your genetic code. In short, cells have two instruction books: one, chapter and verse on how to do its assigned specialty, and two, information on all the fine points of every other cell's specialty. Information sharing is total. A small minority of biologists assumes there are some blind spots, but so far there is not a single gap within the body.

However, if the connection is off-kilter, your posture may be compromised, almost always visibly by imbalance and dysfunction. The arrogant, egocentric mind thinks it possesses the power to control reality by the force of intellectual firepower. Although human beings are gifted with capacity for high EQ—"emotional intelligence"—bending reality to our will thanks to our large brains is an illusion. The effort to change your posture without a simultaneous request from the cells of your body brings on a dark cloud of negative emotions—thunderheads of fear, futility, and anger. Why? You are in way over your head, and you know it. The frenetic, calculating "me mind" tries to fix the internal problem when, in fact, no fixing is required. Nothing internal is broken. The cells are fine, but even so, they are put on red alert, revved up to fight the thinking mind's illusory fears. Little by little, the defeats that come from battling the wrong enemies take a damaging toll. Health deteriorates, and the symptoms of dysfunctional posture bear silent witness to that decline.

Poor posture is a symptom—a limitation—or a warning from your body through pain or stiffness. A drooping head, slumping shoulders, and wobbling gait, as well as a host of other characteristics, are confirmation that the mind is too busy sending out frantic SOS messages to find the energy resources needed to keep your musculoskeletal system functions operating up to par. Eventually, it has no other choice but to ring the big gong of pain. The modern, thinking mind—a term I use to distinguish it from the much older, aware, feeling mind—is a worrywart. Perpetually alarmed by the losing struggle to perfectly control reality, the worrying mind bombards the body with hormonal warnings that end up reshaping our musculoskeletal system, and over- and under-revving important internal physiological processes. In turn, anxiety is stoked up even more by the musculoskeletal system's precarious condition, which can include muscular weakness, inflexibility, instability, and severe limitations of function and routine mobility. And we all should know that prolonged, increased anxiety can cause trouble for us.

I used to believe that by returning to good posture, the peace and balance of the aware mind would be simultaneously restored.

My mistake was to regard the absence of pain as the principal requirement. By eliminating pain, I assumed people would continue to eagerly work on recovering their musculoskeletal system to full function because it felt good. I underestimated the power of the thinking mind to remain locked in crisis mode.

But why does a minority of patients escape from such a dire situation? They possess peace of mind securely anchored by the positive energy accessed by an aware mind, which is reinforced and even supported by less-than-perfect posture. Yes, indeed, positive energy can at times counteract imperfect health, because it is a causal source of determination and confidence.

Distilling Emotion from Experience

The first task of this book is to forge a reasonably coherent understanding of the causal link between positive energy, good posture, good health, and the aware mind. Vitality and vibrancy come from peace of mind, which lies deep within our oldest and richest legacy as human beings.

The creation of the experiential pool consists of a series of events that form an experience. This experience expresses meaning through the emotions produced by those who lived through the events and consequently are capable of periodic recollection of both the events and the emotions. Every link in the causal chain represents the impact of energy, regardless of its form, causing external (and internal) change. Awareness is our choice. Likewise, unawareness is too. Either way, experiences and the emotions associated with them have impact moving forward.

If this seems like what circus clowns used to call a Chinese fire drill, give yourself a chance to consider my riff on causality. The relationship between health, emotions, and actions demonstrates the mind-body connection, and our awareness allows us to make conscious choices. So am I saying that choices made from awareness is a good thing? You bet I am.

★ ★ ★ ★ ★

When Marie first came to my Egoscue clinic in Del Mar, California, she made a choice to think of herself as an "overweight, overworked mother" of two children. Her words, not mine. She was thirty-eight years old. Her lower back hurt—big time. A physician had diagnosed the pain as a symptom of a herniated disk. From the way she stood against my office wall, her back flat against its surface, I suspected that she had two herniated disks: one fully herniated, the second just getting started.

I asked her why she had elected to come to see me. She said that a friend had recommended the Egoscue Method because of its reputation for getting fast results. Marie didn't have time for pain. I explained that her spine had lost most of its lower S-curve due to years of sitting in a chair for hours at a time. Consequently, a vertebra in the spine exerted uneven pressure on the disk and walked (that is, nudged or levered) it out of its proper position until a nerve got in the way.

"Can I walk it back in?" she asked.

"No, but you can do the next best thing," I said.

In the first hour, we managed to eliminate about two-thirds of the pain by engaging pelvic muscles that partially restored the S-curve. In effect, we repositioned the spine and got it off the nerve. I gave her a homework "menu" of postural exercise that would take about forty minutes a day to complete. When she left, I wondered if Marie would stick with it or opt for a much faster treatment—surgery—rather than the more time-consuming process of curing her spinal dysfunction through non-invasive methods.

Three weeks and a couple of telephone calls later, Marie was back and she had made another choice: she was no longer "overweight and overworked." Well, maybe she could lose a few pounds, but her harassed, hurry-to-be-buried attitude had changed.

"By getting rid of so much of the pain the first day and the rest a few days later, I realized that all I needed to do was restore my balance by getting aligned and my energy levels would zoom upward. I haven't felt this good in fifteen years."

Marie was relaxed and all smiles. "The results were almost instant. I can feel the energy flowing and percolating from head to foot when I start doing the E-cises."*

I told her she had lost her deer-in-the-headlights look. Marie laughed and said, "Yeah, I was really freaked." What Marie did was to rediscover cause and effect. We humans are designed to engage our sensory (emotional) mechanisms, which link to electrochemical trace data stored in our cells. This data has been preserved in the form of an indestructible pulse of energy. Think of it this way: you eat a candy bar as an afternoon snack. Regardless of whether you bother to read the ingredients on the wrapper, the sugar, cocoa, various coloring agents, preservatives, and artificial flavorings affect—that is, stimulate—a response that you feel immediately or that your body stores for later. In other words, energy is obtained and used to cause change within the body, or it is stockpiled to make a change happen in the future.

The Virtue of Thoughtlessness

We humans know reserved energy as emotions or feelings. If you fished a discarded candy wrapper out of the trash, even if you hadn't eaten the candy, you still would have information about the products stored in your body. Similarly, if you fished a discarded event from your memory banks, you'd find stored-up emotions or

---

* At Egoscue Method clinics, postural therapy comes in the form of "E-cises" that re-engage, re-align, and strengthen musculoskeletal system functions.

emotional subcomponents. Yet what you feel is different from what you think. A memory of an incident we experienced is produced by an electrochemical event stored in the cells as energy. When triggered, or remembered, the feeling announces its origin to the brain and the rest of the body as anger, surprise, or any of a score of familiar expressions of emotion-laden energy. We don't have to think about emotion—it is part of our memory bank, and we feel it. But if you don't know how you feel, your sensory output and perception go unheeded. Hence, making a choice is impossible (if you do choose a blanked-out emotion).

You exist today because your ancestors knew how they felt, took appropriate action, and then stored the information that allowed them to make a similar choice sometime in the future. If you don't know how you feel, beyond being assailed by powerful emotions that are pummeling all of your physiological processes, you're on a tightrope without a safety net. It's time for you to restore your right to choose how you feel. It is a critical step in pain free living.

TWO

THE CALM

DESPITE ALL THE TESTING AND SOPHISTICATED scientific research associated with today's advanced medical treatments, the most reliable way for a doctor to promote healing and full recovery from accidents and chronic disease is to rely on the patient's awareness of how he or she feels.

I know, I know. Feeling has been made to seem pretty wimpy. In reality thousands of internal super-systems preside over this realm of our being. Nothing slips by unnoticed. Our inner monitors never shut down, never take a day off. Unfortunately, thousands of years and much ingeniousness have been devoted to learning how to "mute" the resulting cacophony of constant feedback—starting with the old standby "No news is good news."

Don't be so sure. Nonetheless, most of us unwisely settle for contrived distractions and forms of numbed-down stoicism rather than face the incoming daily, hourly, minute-to-minute flow of knowledge that can come from a sophisticated real-time network that is shrugged off as meaningless or only consulted on rare occasions to spare us a little (counterfeit) peace of mind (the origin of our modern penchant for reflexively trusting in experts, an important theme of this book). And there is the opposite extreme that reads the slightest of irritations as a dire, life-threatening disease, a new epidemic; even good news is transformed into a death sentence.

I am an advocate of awareness, not fear.

Awareness. Don't misunderstand. I'm not using the word in any special poetic or spiritual sense. This is totally basic. We can do "awareness." This island of life that harbors us is full of noises, alluring scents, sharp edges, sweet tastes, and shooting stars. Our awareness is a great—quite possibly the greatest—treasure that we possess. It is a survival tool that took us from a precarious perch at the edge of a dark forest to where we are today.

"How are you?" is a serious question. "Fine, thank you" was the preprogrammed default answer until about a hundred years ago, when medical innovation began to take off. (To be fair, it's still a preprogrammed answer in polite conversation, but it shouldn't be if you're talking to a health-care professional.) Before then, to safeguard their health, sensible people had to rely on the body's practicality and flexibility. Things were pretty simple. All he or she needed to do was to pay attention, and then, sooner or later, an obvious change would occur: a strong stomach turned queasy, a long-distance walker started getting blisters on her feet, a hunter's acute hearing faded. In other words, people began to receive warnings featuring *symptoms* that suggested internal alarms or potentially harmful conditions—spiking temperature, inflamed tissue, aching joints, and the like.

I use the word "symptoms" above in italics because the health crisis we find ourselves in today started with a fundamental error involving the identification of symptoms. A symptom does not cause sickness or chronic disease. It is a calling card, a fingerprint, a signpost. It is an indicator of a problem, not the problem itself. Since I assume you want a cure, not just a treatment, you need to be able to tell me about your symptoms. If you can't tell me— and far more important, if you can't tell yourself—how you feel, you risk receiving questionable treatments from your health-care provider. I'm talking about wild pitches that inevitably get wilder and wilder.

Comparison Shopping

Okay, let's pause for a moment while I convince you or reaffirm that your body is nearly perfect. All you need to do is choose a physiological function: digestion or respiration will do, or climbing a set of stairs. To be truly impressed, study reproduction. Spend a couple of hours in the library or on the Internet doing a little research. You will come away, I hope, with the sense that something with so many moving parts, chemical reactions and interactions, synchronicity, and almost impossibly precise timing doesn't tend to make mistakes. True, nature is not without a few flaws—cells might zig instead of zag—but it happens relatively rarely, and nowhere near as often as would be suggested by the mass media's focus on new epidemics, diseases, and doomsday scenarios that have convinced millions of people that their nearly perfect bodies are fragile and genetically prone to break down.*

Like the brain, our other physiological processes have many alternative pathways to choose from to get around obstacles. Medical science has yet to find the exact causes of the marquee killer diseases, such as the many forms of cancer. With fewer symptomatic treatments, which are often damaging and stressful in their own right, and more attention to changing destructive inputs from outside the body, I expect many of those killers will be conquered, and that it will happen soon.

Hire Up

There is just one more important task on the agenda—getting you to come back to work as CEO of your own health. It is up to you to decide what works, what doesn't, and why. You, and you alone, are the foremost health expert.

---

* Only 5 percent of the population is affected by gene defects (Lipton).

Every human being has an incredibly sophisticated array of sensory receptors, yet the incoming messages rarely get over the threshold of conscious awareness. This is not normal; viewed across humankind's million-plus years on Earth, it is very definitely abnormal and extremely dangerous. An inverse relationship has formed with the advances in civilization, education, and technological innovation, drowning out and suppressing what was once a robust stream of understandable, actionable, sensory, internal health guidance that even an unschooled Bronze Age farmer was capable of comprehending and acting upon with a reasonably good chance of success.

Here's the plan: in the first three chapters, my top priorities are to briefly cover what has happened, why, and how you can restore your health awareness. Not a bad way to get started. It puts you in a position to take the steps necessary to reactivate an essential life-support system and resume monitoring the state of your health by receiving clear warnings when there's danger, or getting positive signals in reaction to beneficial circumstances. In short order, you can stop being dependent on others for health expertise.

Am I suggesting you fire the doctor? No, of course not. Instead, resume being your physician's working partner and best resource, the primary supplier of reliable information on the state of your own health. The doctor can make an educated guess about what's going on. You don't need to guess—you can feel it, and more than ever that's what it takes to withstand disease, accidents, and premature aging.

Chapter 2 includes a simple exercise that I urge you to do without delay. Drop everything and get with it. You will feel an important change in your body and mind. The door to your perfect health will start to open.

From there we will go on to consider the musculoskeletal system's role in keeping you on an even keel, fully aware, and energized. I will introduce you to the secret of humankind's evolutionary success as a species: posture. Sounds quaint, eh? Don't be fooled. Our posture announces to the world whether we are strong or weak, growing or declining, living or dying. Posture is an early-warning system, the closest thing to a master key to the door to perfect health. It reacts immediately to change, sends out a cost-benefit analysis, and tells you in unmistakable terms whether you're on the right track or the wrong track. I'll set out three complete daily conditioning programs that will let you get on the track you decide is right for you by re-engaging, strengthening, and re-aligning your magnificent musculoskeletal system. You get to select which program works best and feels best. Not only is this the means to living pain free without toxic drugs and traumatic surgery, it is the foundation of a long lifetime of good health in general.

In Chapter 3, I'll share with you my understanding of the health role positive energy plays. Chronic pain is a symptom of correctable energy deprivation, not human frailty. Luckily, so is poor posture. Posture is visible and can be easily realigned from a dysfunctional state to a functional, positive, energy-generating mode. Good posture is not solely a matter of aesthetics or personal beauty. It is "good" simply because it feels good, and in that way it is a crucial element in the health-awareness feedback system that I'll be discussing.

Also coming up is a smattering of quantum physics, Zen spiritual practices and doctrine, and assorted cutting-edge hypothesizing (like the Law of Attraction, mindfulness, David R. Hawkins' work on the beneficial power of high wavelength energy, and Bruce H. Lipton's book *The Biology of Belief*).

Sense and Sensibility

There are five traditional senses: sight, hearing, smell, touch, and taste. Six others are also generally recognized, among them being balance, awareness of time, sensitivity to temperature, and pain. I believe there are many more, each supported by a sensory system that responds to specific physical stimuli. We are consciously aware of only a few. However, if we could assign a *click* to every incoming stimulus and a *clack* to the outgoing response, there would be a deafening uproar of traffic. Along with the metabolic process, sensory reception and perception may well be the essential operational cornerstones of human biology.

Today modern science—medical science in this case—has diligently claimed responsibility for all but the most superficial aspects of our health. Only a fully licensed, impressively credentialed expert need reply to such questions as "How do you feel?" Or so it seems. The body is just too complicated for average folks to comprehend. Or so it seems.

I have a feeling that down deep you don't buy that, and you're absolutely right not to. The book you are reading is a celebration of our perfect health, and an invitation to retrieve the body's power to heal, to grow, to live a long, joyful life free of limitations and chronic pain.

You and I and the rest of the human tribe know more about our individual health, how we feel, and why we feel it than all the so-called experts combined. That *knowing* is a gift, a legacy that has partially allowed humankind to establish a foothold on this remote speck of the cosmos. Relinquishing such a heritage is unthinkable, yet we are under growing pressure to hand it over to those who sincerely believe themselves to be better informed and better equipped. I'm not bashing doctors or knocking pharmaceutical companies; the blame game is a waste of time and energy. My objective is to reestablish the legitimacy of *How do you feel?* and to once again receive a direct, candid answer—not how the cardiologist or the director of research at Merck thinks you feel—to a question that has more salience than any other you could ask about your health.

Why? Because once you are fully in touch with how you feel, you'll know the right thing to do. So one of the central themes that we will be exploring is this: your body is smarter than you are.

Whoops! Do we need to slam on the brakes and decide where the body stops and where you start? Let's not. For now, proceed as though the physical body and the *you-mind* (a stuffy though useful shorthand for individual consciousness and cognition) are separate entities—they're not, but taking a shortcut here will save time and trouble.

Anyway, the smart body knows when it is sick, what it takes to get well, and how to live a long and happy life. But the body needs a little help from you. Your job is to pay attention and become aware of how the body is constantly changing as it responds to its environment and, when necessary, take appropriate action to support that response.

Equipped with two eyes, ears, hands, feet, and at least five senses, the you-mind takes care of interacting with the extremely variable external environment. In return, your body keeps you informed about what it needs to maintain internal equilibrium, such as having adequate food, water, sleep, shelter, companionship, fun, and the like. If you are inattentive, don't care, or prefer to pass the buck to someone else, be prepared to suffer the consequences. Pain is one way the body communicates this serious information. In the end, by ignoring the body's wisdom you are damaging your health and shortening your life.

You are the only one with total access, literally speaking, to complete inside knowledge on what's really happening to your physiological processes: *your* organs, *your* tissues, *your* cells. The body keeps you completely informed. Medical doctors can make assumptions, and drug companies can research, test, and sell reasonably effective products; only you have the actual *feel* for what works and what doesn't. It is a talent, an inner genius, you were born with.

If you opt out of playing this important role, your health may be in jeopardy. The increasingly complex technology and head-spinning treatment choices might make you feel like you couldn't possibly be the key part of your own health care.

Confusing?—sort of.

Challenging?—sure.

But you're the key. All you need is to be reconnected to the power of perfect health that comes from taking action, and making choices based on knowing the answer to a simple four-word question:

How do you feel?

I know that you know. Now let's explore that knowing together.

Balancing Act

If you've read any of my four previous books, you may remember that I like to encourage the reader to participate in fun and games. Well, here I go again.

Take off your shoes and socks. And stand up. Please.

Read the rest of this paragraph, then shut your eyes and follow these instructions. Stand normally. Relax. Let your feet, shoulders, and head go where they want to go (and do go when someone isn't barking out orders). Keep your feet in place and inhale and exhale a couple of times. Take your time. Notice how your weight is distributed. One leg may be working harder than the other. Is it the right leg? Or is it the left leg? Feel where the weight settles in the feet—is it in the heels? Maybe it's the inside edge, outside edge, or toward the toes. It's likely to be in a different spot for each foot. Let two or three minutes go by. Breathe.

Next, open your eyes. Read some more. Did you notice what was going through your mind when you were analyzing the weight distribution? Was there a jumble of ideas, images, and sensations?

A little of this and that? Quick, arrhythmic bursts of activity? A sensory jigsaw puzzle with a bunch of missing pieces? At the end of this paragraph, close your eyes again and pay attention to your mental traffic. Give it a minute and reopen your eyes.

Now, I'd like you to distribute your weight evenly. Read this paragraph and close your eyes again. Stand with both feet roughly parallel, pointing straight ahead and about hips-width apart. Now, turn them inward a little, until they are slightly pigeon toed. Easy does it. Carefully swing your torso, shoulders, and head around until you can feel the weight move in your feet.

Did you ever play flashlight tag as a kid? The beam of light moves like a disk, right? Your weight will have the same characteristic: it will focus and slide here and there. Nudge the disks into the balls of your feet. Bob a little at the knees, and tweak your hips. Some people will really have to crank themselves around. It may feel strange, precarious. Believe me, though, when the weight rests over the balls of the feet, your posture is in a balanced position. (Contortions and muscular effort to hold you there are necessary because your musculoskeletal structure is fighting to pop out of the temporary alignment I've put you in.) When you get the weight centered, notice how it feels, and notice what your mind is doing. Go ahead, try it.

When we have clients perform the same exercise in one of our Egoscue Method clinics, most of them say that in the first unbalanced position their minds are whirling, jumpy, and chaotic. They feel troubled, uncertain, uneasy. Balanced, however, is a different story. The mind calms down. It loses the jittery quality. There's more steadiness and clarity.

By changing your posture, you've changed your mind. The result is similar to switching channels on a radio or TV. A distant signal wavers and breaks up; adjusted to a closer, stronger frequency, the transmission sharpens and settles down.

Vis Viva ("Living Force")

You are 100 percent energy. All matter, from rocks to race-horses, is the permutation of energy. Consequently, you are indestructible because energy cannot be destroyed. Forms do change, though. For instance, Shakespeare has been dead for about four hundred years, yet all of his energy is still around. There is a chance, though maybe small, that some of it was incorporated into your corporal being—part of an ear lobe or skin tissue—because matter-energy is infinitely recyclable. Prior to residing within the thumb of the bard's right hand, matter-energy could have been a freckle on King Tutankhamun's chin.

No one knows how energy is channeled into a particular form or how to positively distinguish between a genius' energy and an earthworm's. In its vast variety, energy is the cosmic equivalent of chicken soup—a delicious cure-all elixir. The energy in the average adult human would explode with the force of thirty large hydrogen bombs (7 by 10^{18} joules of potential energy, according to Bill Bryson, who I'm trusting to get it right, since a calculation like that is several hydrogen bombs' worth of intellectual firepower beyond my meager capabilities), but so far we are able to release only a tiny percentage of it in one burst.

Am I saying that your thought process will change along with your posture? Most people who practice the techniques in this book report a calming, clarifying effect, which indicates that that is probably happening. With restored posture, our brains are able to provide a smoother, less hassled ride. By not skidding on icy patches and by avoiding clunking into potholes, our whole physiological state is more tranquil, less stressed, better grounded. In short, we *feel* better.

So, standing around with your eyes closed playing a form of flashlight tag with your postural weight distribution is a big deal?

Actually, it is.

What you've just done is bridge the gap between mortality and immortality. Yes, that's right—because we are more than flesh and blood, more than skin and bones. We are energy. Our understanding of physics tells us that energy is indestructible.

The exercise gives us a window on the process that makes all human beings as indestructible as a block of granite. Of course, granite can be ground into sand over the long haul, and eventually the grains of sand are reduced to molecules of matter. Because all matter is energy, those molecules are destined to return to the vast power surge of waves and particles created by the big bang, where they pulse and pummel, push and pull across an infinity of space and time.

If achieving postural balance calms the mind, it is reasonable to assume that it also beneficially affects our other physiological systems—all of them. And that is precisely my assumption and the assumption of this book. On my weekly radio show, I was fond of torturing the listeners by singing bits and pieces of the old gospel song "Them Bones"—"the knee bone's connected to the thigh bone, the thigh bone's connected to the hip bone . . . ," and so on. The musculoskeletal system's connections extend from head to foot. Its circuitry wires together the whole body and, what's more, links it to a vast field of high-wavelength energy that radiates from one end of the cosmos to the other (except that most physicists believe the cosmos, or whatever you choose to call it, has no beginning and no end).

Keep in mind that increased mass contributes to resistance, drag, friction, and heat. Heat is a variety of radiation, and radiation affects molecular movement. Also, mass is a function of structural form, and forms vary in the way mass is expressed, from thin and easily penetrated to dense and impermeable. This range is found in the human musculoskeletal system too—in tissues that range from functional and balanced (energy-permeable) to dysfunctional and unbalanced (energy-impermeable).

What our version of flashlight tag reveals is that we are not passive bystanders at the cosmic energy Olympics, but that our mortal bodies are designed to deliberately tap into and draw from the vast supply of energy to fuel our health. Furthermore, we now know how to do it—and it's easy!

Plug and Play

To visualize the role of the musculoskeletal system by using an everyday analogy, think about how your TV set is connected to its power source: cord→plug→wall outlet→household wiring→electricity pole→electrical grid, and so on. If you were to step on the plug at the end of your TV's power cord—really tromp on it—the prongs of the plug would probably bend to the point that they'd no longer fit properly into the wall outlet. The TV wouldn't work. Or the plug might make a loose connection that would cause the set to flicker on and off.

Your musculoskeletal system is like household wiring, a connector of your individual nerves to the universal energy supply. The strength of that connection—the total volume of the incoming flow of energy—depends on postural balance. In other words, energy flow is determined by the way mass is arranged structurally. The more balanced you are, the more energy moves with less friction along the conduit and through the plugs. Those who are fully balanced receive an unrestricted flow of high wavelength energy because there are fewer obstructions in the mind and body. A minor imbalance means that the energy inflow is slightly impeded. But a person with severe imbalance, or someone who is stooped, with his head down, shoulders rounded forward, feet shuffling, and with drastically limited movement, is losing out on almost all of the available high-quality energy.

The plug is barely making contact—his "TV set" is flickering and threatening to go dark.

By being balanced to slightly off-balance, you have a steady flow of almost all the high-wavelength energy needed to lead an active, deeply satisfying life. Those who are badly out of balance are on the brink of shutting down. Their physiological systems, from the innermost organs to the outermost bones, muscles, and joints, are collapsing.

At one time, possibly as recently as seventy to a hundred years ago, most people were in postural balance or close to it. The people in old photographs are more likely to stand with readily apparent correct posture. Those who were imbalanced were still largely intact and capable of rebounding with relatively minor adjustments in their activity levels. Theirs was an environment that required motion. Routine, everyday, musculoskeletal movement brought them closer to balance without much deliberate effort. Today, for a majority of the population of the economically advanced regions of the world, balance is on the wane as the high-tech environment demands less and less motion due to desk jobs and labor-saving technology. At the same time, and not at all coincidentally, there is a growing health crisis. Medical costs are soaring, the news media regularly panics about new epidemics, and severe, chronic pain and lost mobility are becoming commonplace along with increasingly invasive treatments to treat them.

I'm concerned, but not worried—and you shouldn't worry either. Human health is a well-marked, two-way street that can take us to a long, deeply satisfying life free of chronic pain, limitation, and fear—if we make a relatively simple, straightforward commitment to retaining and sustaining our legacy of postural balance. We can travel in the wrong direction on that two-way street, and we are. Presently, humankind is losing postural balance and underlying health, but what is lost can be found again. I believe we can turn this around quickly once we put our minds—our aware minds—to it. That's the lesson of the exercise that I've shared with you in this chapter. Please try it again, and share it with your family and friends.

★   ★   ★   ★   ★

The starting place to a quick turnaround is to recognize that the body's amazing arrangement of muscles, bones, and nerves made an important contribution to our development as a species, continues to define us as individuals, and has a major, major, major influence on our overall health and happiness.

THREE

YOUR FUEL GAUGE

NOT THAT I'M BRAGGING, but I don't look my age—and neither do you. Both of us are 13.7 billion years old, give or take 200 million.

We are built to last, literally constructed out of debris: space junk, to be blunt. You and I have the good fortune to be nothing less than 100 percent energy produced at the creation of the universe.

Who we are varies from person to person; what we are is the ultimate in basic material. Energy *is*—it just is. It doesn't grow, procreate, subdivide, or pop out of a magic lamp. It simply exists, and is neither newly concocted nor in danger of being destroyed. Energy can move from place to place (or remain in place), and be changed from one form to another. In the process, energy performs work, exclusively as motion or movement. You—that is, as kinetic energy, without an ego, a face-lift, and a fashionable zip code—will always exist, be on the move, and be at work (unless you are stored or *potential* energy, and then you'll get a break from work until you become kinetic energy again).

In the Beginning

"Creation" has become a loaded word. Created when, we may ask, by whom or by what? Were we created by God; the big bang; the teeny, tiny bubbles of the primordial swamp; or something else? Take your pick. If you believe that the big bang was the source of all creation, then the age of the universe is estimated to be about 14 billion years, when what scientists call a "singularity"—finite matter so dense it compacted down into infinitely dense matter—suddenly exploded.

The Bubble universe attempts to account for the pre-bang existence of so-called infinitely dense matter derived from finite matter. Basically, it means that a foam or froth, stirred up by energy fluctuation in a parent universe, formed a tiny bubble that grew until it accumulated enough mass to spin off galactic structures and eventually life-forms, either before or after a sudden, huge expansion.

The bubble-and-bang process probably adds another 15 billion years or more to the age of our universe. It is guesswork, however. Thanks to astronomer Edwin Hubble, we now "know" that all matter in space has been proportionately expanding from one single flash point or event. Theologians have their own time lines. The Torah, or the Judaic holy book, for example, puts the age of the universe at about 5,760 years.

So, in a very real sense, we are all in the same big boat. We are like Dalande, the ghost in Richard Wagner's opera *Der Fliegende Holländer*, doomed to sail forever.

From an energy standpoint, we're all on a very long voyage. If the concept of immortality does not appeal to your sensibilities, would it suit you to have eighty, ninety, or a hundred years or more of perfect health? Energy tosses the whole idea of chronic disease and aging right out the window. Energy doesn't get sick or old. Energy moves, yet there are no moving parts like those in a clock or an internal combustion engine, no sprockets and levers that can wear out or break. Instead, there are various expressions of energy, some working one way, some another. For example, when you digest breakfast, this stokes the cellular ATP boiler that converts the bacon and eggs into adenosine 5'-diphosphate, the metabolic fuel used to power the body's cells. Meanwhile, others are busy repairing your stockpile of various specialized proteins—perhaps twenty thousand per cell—which undergo heavy wear and tear from basic tasks such as muscular contraction and respiration. Nothing is broken, diseased, or wrong; energy is merely doing its job in various anatomical and physiological structures. This work includes building, maintaining, and animating the body's structures, since energy was involved in their creation in the first place. A constant interplay of action and reaction takes place as particles, waves, forces, and force fields carom off one another; become ripples, torrents, and tsunami; raise and lower temperatures; set fires, and trigger chemical reactions and combinations that even the maddest of mad scientists couldn't dream up.

Close Resemblance

I am going to use a pocketful of metaphors to explain what happens to the energy in our bodies.

Matter tends to be both pushy and sticky. By "pushy," I mean that it can use the equivalent of head-butts to abruptly alter the status quo. Particle energy collides with or zooms past slow-moving matter (and sometimes slips around loosely packed molecules and runs straight through without making contact), which tends to bring on a quick, dramatic reorganization of the neighborhood in which it's traveling. Imagine a toddler pouncing into the middle of a flock of feeding pigeons. To understand "sticky," think of objects that have mass attraction to one another. The greater the mass, the greater the attraction.

Gravitational attraction acts as a glue between newly arriving energy to existing matter, layer by layer. This sort of attraction encourages the creation of many different forms of matter and can help transform a stagnant, primordial puddle, for instance, into a chowder teeming with life. Billions of years of pushy and sticky churned up these ingredients, combined with extreme temperatures and pressure to help jump-start single-celled life-forms.

Energy vibrates by moving through space in zigs and zags, like the teeth of a serrated knife. There are sharp peaks and narrow valleys—the steeper and deeper the declivities, the more potent the energy. In other words, the serrated blade is sharper because the cutting edge is longer and moves faster and more efficiently. There may be hundreds more peaks and valleys. Ultra-high-wavelength energy zooms past low-wavelength energy because sluggish energy has negligible gravitation attraction. It may twitch or throb but doesn't solidly bond to the incoming energy. Its mass is too spongy.

All life prospers or perishes as a result of its ability to make productive use of this swirl of energy. The failure rate is high. Eventually everything that lives dies—yet its energy is here, there, and everywhere to stay. Meanwhile, extinction—the wholesale elimination of particular life-forms—seems to be in the cards. In the short run, fewer than one-tenth of 1 percent have made the cut since life on Earth began about four billion years ago. There have been millions—one estimate is 30 billion—of now-you-see-them-now-you-don't species, many lasting seconds and a relatively few others holding on for centuries. Today, estimates of the number of living species of plants, insects, animals, and "organic others" (not counting all the tiniest of the tiny multitude of micro-organisms) range upward from five to thirty million. The as-yet-undead are extraordinarily, and improbably, lucky to have lasted so long.

The casualties all lost the ability to change internally, a non-negotiable requirement that allows for the continual accommodation of the fluctuating external flow of incoming energy. For a while, reproduction and hereditary gene transfer go on, though it is more than likely that the processes are gradually compromised until systemic equilibrium and viability weaken and collapse.

The premature aging and death of an individual are similar to the extinction of an entire species. John, for instance, was a high-powered Washington lobbyist who, in his twenties and thirties, managed the stress of his demanding professional life by running every morning and working out at the gym several times a week. He loved his routine—for good reason. Incoming energy (stress, including fatigue, cellular damage, and other ramifications of a toxic lifestyle) was counteracted by the release of internal energy stored in the muscles, which boosted John's heart rate, metabolism, and cell replacement cycle. In other words, by working out regularly, John deliberately made an internal change take place. His physiological systems were working smoothly in balance. Yet, for some reason— "too busy" is the usual suspect—he started cutting back on running and visits to the gym. Gradually, there was more incoming stressful change and less internal balancing change. Cells died at a higher and higher rate, their efficiency declined, and subtle alterations of all of his physiological processes took place. John started to feel the effects, so he resorted to vodka to adjust his internal chemistry. Drinkers think they are imbibing to make merry or to unwind, yet what they are actually doing is desperately fiddling with their body fluids. Ethanol is matter; hence, it is energy. However, not much work is accomplished by drinking alcohol, other than a quick alteration of mood and, more insidiously, an interference in oxygen intake, blood composition, and liver function. As a result, stress gets the upper hand. The cumulative imbalance from incoming change swamped John's health. He died of colon cancer at the age of fifty-two.

Last Resort

Millions of women and men like John prematurely age, sicken, and die because their health loses balance and is unable to bring about routine internal changes that once took place in the course of daily life. Historically, when bad weather wiped out an important food crop, business as usual came to a halt: people migrated, ate grass-hoppers, or plundered their neighbors. When all else failed, they starved. Change—behavioral change—was imperative, and they knew it.

Even so, some changes are out of reach, which may be the very reason dinosaurs became extinct. There is convincing evidence that a gigantic dust cloud, kicked up when a meteor the size of Times Square slammed into the Earth, probably doomed large dinosaurs by blotting out the sun's rays. The lack of sun killed plants, which in turn killed plant-eating animals, and so on up the food chain. The voracious reptiles were unable to change their internal requirement for readily available calories. Adios, *T. Rex*.

But other forms of life did change and survive. In such cases, a change in behavior was involved. When John changed by giving up running and working out, he was really acting like a giant, bad-tempered reptile with a tiny brain. He kept stressing his body, provoking the need for internal change, and stopped providing precisely the kind of behavioral response that accomplishes the necessary internal change. Why? Not stupidity. My answer is that John allowed himself to be distracted by a modern lifestyle that drowns out the most essential messages delivered by his senses—for example, important news flashes such as: *This feels good, keep it up! That feels bad, stop right now!*

Not only was John smart enough to know that running and reasonably strenuous and varied, regular physical workouts were the right things to do, his posture supplied graphic evidence just in case he was not thinking straight, not receiving the sensory messages. The stiff joints and short-windedness he experienced after giving up his exercise routine were handwriting on the wall, but he misread the message. They were signs all right, but not of aging.

Nature rewards efficiency and punishes inefficiency. Gathering infirmity for weeks, months, and years is colossally inefficient. What is the point of wasting valuable resources—food, fresh water, and shelter—on someone who is weak and soon headed for the grave? On the contrary, sudden death by way of accidents and plagues of virulent disease are far more rational in that the fewer mouths to feed, the better. Logic strongly suggests, therefore, that humans were built for either a very long life or a very short one. The vain among us may scoff, but facial wrinkles do not mean that the end is near; however, a dysfunctional, collapsing musculoskeletal system usually does. Posture is the equivalent of the gasoline gauge in the dashboard of a car. A quick glance revealed to our early ancestors who among them was fit to fight, bear and nurture children, and work hard enough to prosper in the face of adversity.

John could feel his good health draining away. He could see it as well. Unfortunately, the lobbyist who never forgot a face couldn't remember what his deteriorating posture meant. Just as a building verges on collapse when its load-bearing floors and walls slump, tilt, and buckle, the musculoskeletal system that loses its horizontal and vertical structures is teetering on the edge of disintegration. Without symmetrical muscular support our essential, gravity-defying, ninety-degree angles give way, leaving the head, shoulders, hips, and knees wobbling, grinding, and gyrating until smooth, strong, spontaneous movement becomes more and more difficult. When posture is no longer fully erect, balanced, flexible, aligned, and well supported by strong muscles from head to foot, the entire physiological package is flatlining. Breathing is compromised, the heart works harder, the colon struggles. Everything gets disrupted.

John regarded his slow-motion, cataclysmic collapse as a natural consequence of living a stressful three or four decades. His unschooled but eminently observant ancient ancestors would have looked at a brother or sister in the same condition and begun setting aside firewood for a funeral pyre.

The Objectivity Myth

As a community, humankind has been getting smarter, more knowledgeable, even wiser about its energy heritage, but it has taken more than seven thousand years. As early as 5000 BCE, spiritual practitioners in what we today call India recognized that *Prana*, a form of energy, an invisible and powerful life force, is a central causal fact of existence. Notice I didn't suggest that the gurus "discovered" or "invented" Prana. Human beings, ancient and modern, inherently know and trust energy because they can feel its vitality without intermediation or indoctrination, and they are capable of full awareness of its gifts. From time to time, however, the thinking mind—possessed of a tendency to upstage the feeling mind—sets out to dethrone energy on the grounds that it is not objective.

If your mother says she loves you, you may take it at face value, but Western science demands proof in the form of carefully defined, observable standards of verification that remain true in all cases. Proof doesn't resort to opinion, bias, or emotion. We're taught to deal in cold, hard facts, even if those facts clash with personal experience or gut instinct. In other words, the *objectivists* have gone outside of themselves by ignoring the feel (the personal emotional content) of what they're directly experiencing. Instead, they attempt to evaluate their own experiences by secondhand criteria endorsed and prescribed by committees of researchers.

From about the mid-seventeenth century to the mid-twentieth century, Western society was hung up on using a clock or some other intricate mechanical contraption as a model—an *object* serving as an *objective* standard—to explain how most things worked, including human health. Newtonian science looked at the world and saw the equivalent of whirring sprockets, wheels within wheels, springs that sprang, and levers that lifted, all governed by laws and forces that could be mathematically plotted and summoned to objectively explain the deepest mysteries.* Seen from this perspective, the world is the sum total of its many component parts. But to understand any complex natural phenomenon you have to take it apart and keep taking the parts apart until you come to the smallest bits of matter, which behave predictably based on their position in space, their mass, and their velocity.

Brainiac

Isaac Newton, 1642–1727, formulated the law of gravitation. Newton's *The Mathematical Principles of Natural Philosophy* is often regarded as the most influential book ever written. It showed how a universal force, gravity, applied to all objects in all parts of the universe, and how it also formulated the three laws of motion.

Newton laid the groundwork for classical mechanics, which is the basis of modern engineering. He was far and away the leading scientist in Britain and Europe by the late 1600s.

What the Newtonians didn't count on was that small just keeps getting smaller. In due course, quantum physicists detected matter so minuscule, it behaved not like a clock, but like something that had the feel—a highly subjective feel—of energy: entangled beams of light, swarms of molecular fragments, and torrents of disobedient

---

* Newton was not necessarily a Newtonian—he was way too smart for that. The clock metaphor would probably have struck him as simple-minded. Lesser mortals needed an intellectual crutch to understate what the great man meant by terms like "acceleration," "velocity," "friction," "position," and the like.

subatomic matter that defy objective science by acting like waves when they are supposed to be particles, and vice versa. Eventually, scientists discovered that matter shrank until it entirely disappeared, only to instantly reappear thousands of miles away and challenge Albert Einstein's twentieth-century contention that nothing travels faster than the speed of light. Predictability went out the window; quantum theorists started concocting outlandish ideas that they admitted couldn't be proven. Suddenly, Prana didn't seem so crazy after all.

Health Awareness

Sleeping when we are tired, eating when we are hungry, and subtly modifying our diet to counteract nutritional deficiencies (a summer of leaner fish in the place of winter's fattier red meat) are vestiges of our subconscious, instinctive, self-adjusting health awareness.

The widespread use of electricity disrupted our awareness of our own health, including our sleep patterns. Meanwhile, processed foods and beverages began to manipulate our sensory perceptions of what we eat. Excessive amounts of salt, fat, and sweeteners are shamelessly used to trick people into making unhealthful choices. Widespread obesity is not an illness—it is evidence of a crime. Does that mean I think we should lock up all the evil food producers? No. We need to return to our health awareness and stop eating their harmful products.

The way the body operates can be compared to a clock, but in modern medical terms, it is akin to a malfunctioning Timex in need of an expert watchmaker. Why? One reason is that the medical establishment has a vested interest in its own success. Like any other industry, to be successful, medicine needs customers—that is, people who believe in the expertise of their doctors.

In addition, human beings are superb toolmakers. Since the invention of the hammer and the wheel, we have employed new tools to extend our control of the environment and to reshape reality. Like Archimedes' lever and fulcrum, our innovative tools move the world by doing what had once been impossible. Micro-medicine, whether it is diagnostic, surgical, or pharmaceutical, thrives on new tools. The notion of fixing or replacing defective body parts as the way to good health grew very slowly, but eventually it took hold. What initially seemed impossible became likely, and even more important, seemed necessary.

Over time, thanks to humankind's tool-making talents, there was a reduction in work effort. There was less walking, stooping, carrying loads, climbing, vigorous hand-and-arm engagement, and the rest of the physical repertoire that had once taken men, women, and children through a full range of motion each day. In its place came an increasingly settled, prosperous toolmaking culture, with each successive generation quietly losing small though vital amounts of musculoskeletal system balance.

Knock, Knock

Physicians are probably dumped on more than any other elite profession, with the possible exception of lawyers. This is in contrast to the respect people had in an earlier era toward men with a black bag—and a smaller number of women, many of them midwives. The affection for likeable, empathetic, less-is-more medicos who made house calls lives on as nostalgia, for the old-time country doc's most powerful medicines were his listening skills, gentle common sense, patience, and bedside manner. This contrasts with the current images of a physician, which tend to be more synonymous with impersonal standards of care and invasive methods of treatment.

What happens when balance goes? There is less energy available to grow, maintain, and sustain the body; physiological systems are under more and more stress; chronic health problems multiply; and the instinctive awareness of the body's health needs is drowned out by fear.

After many years, fear eventually opened the door to Newtonian medical science becoming the dominant Western health-care model. The toolmakers joined forces with the watchmakers. Fearful, running low on energy thanks in part to rapid urbanization and massive industrialization, our ancestors' thinking minds prevailed over their feeling minds. They began to think the body was like all machines, made up of smaller and smaller parts that were prone to breaking down. If experts were needed to build, run, and repair the mechanical marvels that moved freight, milled grain, and loomed textiles, it followed logically that experts were needed to rebuild, repair, and run the human health machine. Non-experts stepped aside to allow those with specialized knowledge and training in *objective* medical science to take over. Thus did once-lowly shamans and herbalists, midwives and barbers, tinkers, alchemists, and quacks evolve into educated, respected, wealthy, and licensed members of the ruling elite.

A combination of engineering and alchemy sprang up to replace a more passive form of medical care that had been practiced by a quasi-priesthood at ease with miracles (not to mention a willingness to foist off cheap tricks for the sake of a quick profit) and an emphasis on spiritual healing as a foundation for physical well-being.

Newtonian Overlap

For a time, the new tools and the procedures in medicine co-existed with human awareness. Doctors were in short supply; the average person rarely saw one. And why bother? The body's own predisposition to cure and care for itself prevailed more often than not, and the placebo effect helped save many who otherwise would have been killed by bumbling apprentices. As trial-and-error experience accumulated, crude, superficial, and relatively benign medical technology was wielded by many kind and prudent men and women who knew better than to risk overly drastic treatment. They gave medicine a good name. But as medical practitioners learned how to control pain, blood loss, and infection, the techniques grew bolder and more invasive. By the mid-nineteenth century, a quick march was underway toward a dominant and domineering Newtonian model.

At the same time, the manual labor required in an agrarian culture —digging, plowing, reaping, lifting, carrying, weaving, and building cottages or castles—gave way to the Industrial Revolution, with its heavier reliance on mechanical tools that emphasized less sustained physical movement, and therefore decreased strength and endurance. A shovel, for instance, is a hand tool—and a high-tech one in its first days—that helped the hands dig deeper holes faster, but powerful muscles and coordination were still essential to its proper use. A steam shovel, on the other hand, does the digging while the operator sits and moves levers and foot pedals. Fewer (and different) muscles are involved; the close interaction of joints, nerves, and physiological processes, including metabolism and respiration, changes in both minor and major ways.

Until the Industrial Revolution, manpower and womanpower did the work. In other words, the movement of the human body produced energy. In just a few decades, technology changed that, liberated humankind from drudgery, and started a de-conditioning process that has drastically affected human health. Urbanization and industrialization have eliminated at least 50 percent of the muscular and skeletal movement that was once routine. Overcrowding and primitive conditions were indeed factors in causing devastating outbreaks of diseases like bubonic plague, but urban dwellers were threatened by another scourge: lack of motion.

By chasing after smaller and smaller physiological components, systems, and processes deemed to be diseased and defective, the latter-day Newtonians set off an explosion of costly medical technology that promises to make the care it offers us as unaffordable as it is dangerous. Your body, ever aware, even if your thinking mind is not, is still trying to make itself heard.

War and Peace

What I am suggesting is to "feel" your way toward musculoskeletal system balance and move away from the broken-clock analogy. I believe you can do it because I have done it myself and now know the incredible peace of mind of good health. I have helped many other people make the same journey.

The very fact that you are still reading this book indicates that you are evaluating my message by the "feel" of it rather than just the "think" of it. In terms of the thinking mind, Newton was a brilliant conceptualizer and abstract thinker. But your body is even smarter. It won't let you die without fully deploying its genius for survival.

I almost wrote, "It won't let you die without a fight," but I don't feel comfortable with health-as-warfare metaphors. The body is far too wise to seek war. It goes toward peace—a state that can be achieved only by postural balance.

···· FOUR ····

FEAR AND LIMITATION

═══════════════════════════════

So, HOW DO YOU FEEL?

Take a moment to think about it. Better yet, put thinking aside and be *aware of how you feel*. Forget for a moment about your thinking mind and what you might have been taught about observation. Instead, try to get an accurate reading of your feelings—that is, your body's responses to stimuli. It's not necessary to minutely scrutinize, measure, or judge what's going on. Just notice; pay attention without imposing meaning, judgment, or coming to conclusions. Find this incoming stream and let it go to work on your perceptions. In due course, you'll rediscover how to distinguish the meaningful high-energy input from the meaningless background noise of second-guessing.

On Your Mind

Conscious thought—storing, retrieving, and prioritizing experiences, including secondhand experiences, with the explicit goal of solving a problem or influencing an outcome—is probably no more than fifty or sixty thousand years old as a common human trait. Prior to that, it seems likely that conscious thought was basic memory retrieval.

Setting an Evolutionary Speed Record . . .

Conscious thought has almost entirely supplanted awareness as the prevailing operational state of the mind. Awareness still remains fully functional and functioning in the background, however. An emergency or anything else that provokes emotional turmoil can bring awareness to the forefront: "I didn't think about it. I just rushed into the burning building." If this function didn't exist, the thinking mind would continually control events.

Freed from the domination of the thinking mind, the aware and feeling mind can keep you anchored in the moment as it receives and responds to the present panoply of stimuli. Stimuli are charged with living, positive, high-wavelength energy, as opposed to negative energy, such as the forces of obstruction and destruction sought by the thinking mind. Awareness isn't passive; rather, it is a grateful acceptance of enlightenment generated by unfiltered and undistorted perceptions. I'll have more to say about negative energy as we go forward. For the moment, to get a taste of negative energy, close your eyes and slowly, with emphasis, say aloud: "Failure, catastrophe, ruin, lies." Pause for a moment to let the meaning sink in. Notice your mood darkening. Negative energy is smothering your enthusiasm and hope.

Once you have located a feeling, describe it. Be both general and specific. If there is pain, is it tenderness or tightness? Does the pain move around or change in intensity? Does it seem to come from muscles, nerves, or joints? Summarize with a word or two: "concentrated," "weak," "sluggish," "intermittent," whatever. "Don't know" may be a cop-out. Sometimes it can be an honest reading, yet usually it means "I know but I don't want to face up to reality; hiding out in dreamland is more comforting." Examine "don't know" very carefully. As Winston Churchill said, "Facts are better than dreams"—and far better than nightmares.

Take a stab at identifying feeling; the more you practice, the more confidence you'll gain.

How Do You Feel?

Take a few notes. Keep a journal, as it can help you stay in practice and fine-tune your ability to be aware of your feelings. Write down how you'd *prefer* or *intend* to feel—you have a lot of choices. For example, I never feel bad. I make a deliberate choice to feel good. I may have a cold or be tired, but I insist on my right to treat each new day as an opportunity for enjoyment and satisfaction.

Einstein, the renowned physicist, once said the most important life decision we make is deciding whether existence is essentially good or essentially bad. How do *you* intend to feel today?

What Do You Expect?

When I ask a new Egoscue Method client how she feels and get a shrug in reply, it tells me that I am dealing with a person who does not feel good and doesn't expect to feel good either. How much of that feeling is self-inflicted by way of expectation? Plenty. Thoughts are things. They exist as energy, and as such they generate force, heat, and momentum. The direction of that momentum is largely up to you.

Frequently, a client will tell me about how much his back or knee hurts. I'll recommend a small postural adjustment. "How do you feel now?"

"It hurts."

"Really? Right now?"

"Well . . . not right now. The pain has gone away. But it'll come back."

"So, the answer is: your back doesn't hurt right now?"

"Yeah," they reluctantly admit, though in their mind, expecting to be in pain amounted to the practical equivalent of actually being in pain.

And that brings us to the notorious "placebo effect." Several studies show that anywhere from 30 percent to 50 percent of the participants in certain experimental drug-testing programs experienced improvement in their medical conditions after receiving doses of inert pharmacological compounds. "Inert pharmacological compounds" means they were concocted from ingredients that were nothing more than sugar, simple starches, and water, for instance, packaged and presented to resemble a drug. Some skeptics dismiss the phenomenon as the scientific equivalent of UFO sightings: random outbreaks of localized, collective lunacy. Others, including me, believe that anticipated benefits aroused by the comforting trappings of medical care—pill bottles and white coats, care versus despair, hopeful action instead of fearful inaction—are powerful enough to improve the health of roughly a third to a half of those tested. Hence, expectation may amount to effectuation, a process the brain uses to help organize experience and emotion and has the potential impact of improving health problems. It's a "mind over matter" thing.

Could it be that belief changes conditions within the body? Or are the studies all wrong, with 30 percent to 50 percent of all patients faking their illness or recovery? Might there be vast numbers of sick and injured who are simply lucky, or just *unlucky*? If you expect pain in your forty-year-old knees when you take a Sunday run in the park, or expect that a cloudy, winter day will make you glum, there is a very good chance that outcome will conform to your expectation. This strongly suggests that the disease model—the prevailing understanding of what cures and what kills—may be wrong.

I hesitate to say that the body believes. I'm not at all reluctant, however, to point out that the body perceives. And by perceiving belief, a state of mind is generated that can lead to a state of action capable of overcoming great obstacles.

Pain and Purpose

To say that the human body is an extremely sensitive organism is an understatement. Our cells bristle with transmitters and receptors that scan our internal environment and the stimuli we receive from external sources. Nothing goes undetected and reaction is swift. If we expect trouble, our body will mobilize its defensive resources. Consequently, our body feels like a fortress under siege: the gates are closed, rations are scarce, and the guns are loaded and cocked. No wonder we don't feel good!

Fear intensifies physical pain. A typical fear-based response to pain is to hold your breath, which only increases stress by reducing oxygen flow. Another fear-based response is to limit your physical activity. "I don't climb stairs anymore," Leroy told me recently. I asked him why not. "Stairs hurt my knees," he said. But stairs are a piece of cake compared to climbing trees, scrambling up mountains, dancing a jig, bowling, and many other challenges his knees could easily handle. I told Leroy that avoiding stairs would soon mean he'd be avoiding hills, minor inclines, stepping off a curb, or stepping into the shower. By restricting his movement, he would reduce, and eventually lose, his ability to move. Then the pain would probably spread to his hips, lower back, and elsewhere as it dutifully warned Leroy about what he was doing to himself.

Pain is not your enemy. It helps to regard pain as a natural occurrence that serves an important service: it notifies the body of a condition, a state, or a stimulus that is detrimental, ranging from the mildly irritating to the harmful. Immediately rushing to take painkilling medicine without first reflecting on what the pain is telling you is unwise. The pill or potion may ease the pain temporarily—with side effects, because there are always side effects—but whatever it is that caused the pain is still there, only now that you're drugged, you can't feel it. Seek a cure, not just treatment. You have nothing to be afraid of. Nothing.

What exactly is fear? Fear is an extreme form of expectation. Most of what we fear might happen never does, yet we suffer the ill effects of our imaginary expectations as if they had actually come to pass. Stay in the moment: by relearning how to be aware of how you really feel, as opposed to how you expect to feel, you allow your body to summon its full resources and generate accurate assessments of what's really happening. This information can be processed and bounced back to your aware mind in the form of self-confidence, pleasure, and, amazingly enough, perfect health and peace of mind.

Being afraid is part of being human, and fear has its place in our emotional lexicon. Fear is the best of emotions and the worst of emotions. We owe it a special place of honor. Without fear, human beings would probably be extinct. However, fear can be a disease—a killer, the mother of all lethal infections—because it diverts energy away from healthy physiological processes. Organs can be drained of important resources and left terribly vulnerable.

Fear comes in two basic variations: Fear Classic and Fear Lite. Classic is similar to a force of nature, like a lightning bolt. When Fear Classic strikes, it overrides most other physiological functions in the name of survival. It's called fight-or-flight mode. There's a click, and we go to the Fear Classic channel without further ado.

Fear Lite is a compact, specialized, and user-friendly mutation of Fear Classic—a Hammond organ compared to a Wurlitzer. Fear Lite plays a mean blues, dirges, funk, gangsta rap, and a host of other emotionally negative tunes that make us feel threatened, uneasy, and troubled but not blasted into the realm of fight-or-flight.

Fear Classic used the prospect of sudden and almost certain death, the *motivator extraordinaire*, to keep our earliest ancestors from being served as lunch before they had a chance to take over the world. Fear Lite was established, through natural selection, as a teaching tool. Unfortunately, it became a mainstay of the modern, thinking mind to the point that most contemporary men and women have almost forgotten how to reason without turning up the negative soundtrack. How many times have you caught yourself saying any of these things to yourself? *My boss hates me; my co-worker is going to stab me in the back; I could have a heart attack; I can't do this myself; I am not going to make it.*

Fear is as much a ubiquitous feature of the modern era as the cell phone. To put the body into fight-or-flight mode, the perception of danger must cross a far higher emotional threshold than one that would occur in the case of an argument with a neighbor or a confrontation with an enemy from another tribe.

From a practical standpoint, playing defense is cumbersome and tiring. The body is flooded with powerful stress hormones that can damage internal systems such as the immune system when high stress levels are maintained over time.

Fear is particularly dangerous because it locks you out of the present moment and blocks the awareness you need to be in contact with your body. Health-care providers have difficulty breaking through the wall of fear that seals off individuals from the help they desperately need. Fear freezes people and makes them believe that change is impossible, even though comparatively minor changes in lifestyle, habit, nutrition, and hydration have a major impact on the body's well-being.

Going Deeper

Power vs. Force by David R. Hawkins is a valuable introduction to the concepts of positive and negative energy. It is not a quick read but it is well worth the effort.

In my opinion, the "modern epidemics" that the sensation-loving news impresarios chatter about—diabetes, autism, fibromyalgia, obesity, autoimmune disorders, and the like—are primarily consequences of putting the body through the stress of preparing to confront danger. When you are stressed, your blood vessels dilate to absorb more oxygen, fast-twitch muscle fibers are primed, blood pressure increases, the optic nerves rev up, and the kidneys and other vital organs slow down to conserve energy. Fear may be the hydrogen bomb of our emotions: it's a last resort, an over-the-top response to an existential threat. Instead of "going nuclear" once or twice a year as our early ancestors did for survival, we live in an era where the fear button is pushed again and again. Fear is about escape and evasion. It wants you to lie low, slink and scurry, and get wound up over what *could* happen rather than what *is* happening. If you are fearful you expect to be hurt, overwhelmed, or defeated. Whether or not that ever happens doesn't matter. You still suffer the ill effects of those expectations. Humankind now lives, sickens, and dies with the consequences of living daily in fear.

Is this a bleak assessment? Yes, but there is a way out.

When you experience anxiety, go take a walk and you'll see (feel) what I mean. Just focus on putting one foot in front of the other, not worrying about your job, paying your mortgage, or taking care of your aging parents. For just a while, stop rerunning the past (where *could haves, would haves, should haves,* and *might haves* grumble and growl) and rehearsing the future through your head, let the footprints in the sand lead to ground zero. You may just be strolling along a walking path, but your head is on a harmful journey elsewhere. The interlude away from fear can restore the soul and regain postural balance. In the process, you escape the emotional firestorm and rediscover peace of mind. Try it.

If walking isn't an option, try this quick exercise instead. Please stand up. Close your eyes (after reading these instructions, of course) and take a deep breath, but stand without deliberately balancing your weight and aligning your musculoskeletal system the way you did in Chapter 2. All set? Now say the words "It is broken" aloud three times. Pause, take another deep breath, and say "Peace of mind" three times.

Did you notice a difference? Many people do, but some don't. So try it again.

For those who do feel a difference, the first part of the exercise tends to produce low-level tension or an uptick of anxiety. By standing in an unbalanced position, you did not draw extra-high-wavelength energy from the universal power grid that produces feelings of well-being. Instead, you reacted to the energy content of the words you said aloud. If you were muscle-tested—a standard, albeit controversial technique of kinesiology—there would likely be a measurable decrease in muscle strength when you repeated the words "It is broken." In general this is typical of negative words, stressful emotional states, and even substances such as sugar, salt, drugs, and many other things we have subconsciously learned are better to avoid.

The second part of the exercise tends to generate a feeling of calmness with a distinct awareness of inner peace. The muscles express awareness by strengthening slightly when you say the words aloud. Words are things, and things are energy.

Actions vs. Ideas

You must live your ideas. It is not enough to be aware. You must act on that awareness.

Upgrade Your Energy

David R. Hawkins, a pioneering author and researcher, has compiled an extensive glossary of positive words paired with their negative counterparts, which he has cross-tested and ranked numerically according to their "Attractor energy" patterns. Saying the words aloud or just reading them silently produces a measurable response. Higher numbers indicate words with a more beneficial effect. Lower numbers correlate with words that align with lower-frequency energy waves, which deliver far less power.

When you lose musculoskeletal system balance and succumb to fear, your thinking mind is awash in negative words and ideas. Hawkins has demonstrated that like attracts like; negative thoughts lead to a thinking mind (rather than a feeling mind) crammed full of inferior-grade energy that undermines health. Hawkins calls this "Subtractor" or "Subtractive" energy. It explains why self-destructive acts or bad habits are often repeated. The drunk has only low-wavelength energy and therefore pours another drink; the liar cannot tell the truth because he doesn't have enough Attractor energy to beat back the easy falsehood.

Hawkins believes that you can upgrade your energy quality by consciously choosing positive, life-affirming ideas and actions—for instance, "giving" draws high-wavelength energy that lifts the human spirit, whereas "taking" does not. I agree. But it is a difficult word-by-word uphill climb that is ultimately doomed to failure unless you restore musculoskeletal system balance and reestablish full high-wavelength energy.

As you discovered while doing the simple exercise in this chapter, it's possible to get a small uptick in peace of mind simply by using positive words aloud (or in thoughts).

However, it is a small trickle of high-quality energy. You can do a lot better than that by changing your posture and restoring balance.

FIVE

MUSCLE MAGIC

MANY EXPERTS SUGGEST THAT HUMANS rose above other beasts because of our brains. But I believe that we owe our special "alpha mammal" status to our musculoskeletal system.

Mere muscle and bone, connecting tissue, jointure, and a gossamer neural tapestry put you into an upright position, balanced on two feet. It allows you to walk, run, turn to the left and right, spin around, reach out and up, use your hands to throw baseballs and snowballs, make love, pray, write sonnets, wage war, and sign peace treaties. I could go on and on. In terms of sheer variety, the human repertoire of locomotion is indeed extraordinary.

Muscle: Part 1

Muscles have two major functions: They contract (the fibers shorten) and relax (the fibers lengthen). No other tissue in the body does this. The result is motion: an ability to accomplish an immense number and variety of tasks, activities, and acrobatics.

Skeletal muscles move bones because they are attached to bones at both ends of a muscle via tendons (the "attachment" or origin, closest to the spinal axis, and the "insertion," which is farther from the axis). By shortening its fibers, a muscle draws the bone near the insertion and toward the anchor and the body's spinal axis.

And yet unlike our other major physiological arrangements, the musculoskeletal system gives the impression (a misimpression, for sure) of being rather haphazard, even crude in function and form—too many moving parts, flat spots, and low-tech compromises. To most students of human anatomy, once you've seen one small intestine, you've pretty much seen them all. The same goes for healthy lungs and hearts: humans have more or less the same collection of conduits, bellows, filters, and pumps. However, the musculoskeletal system comes in a variety of homely shapes and sizes—and not because of sloppy quality control or crude design. I can offer at least two good reasons. One, it operates in a far more eclectic external environment than any other physiological system and, two, the musculoskeletal system provides the means of locomotion for individuals who differ widely in weight, height, muscular strength, stamina, habits, and activity levels.

Muscle: Part 2

To move bones back to their starting points, the muscle that made the initial movement possible relaxes and allows its opposing muscle to contract and therefore return the bones to their resting positions.

By working in pairs, muscles alternate between contracting-relaxing and relaxing-contracting to, for example, allow the body to bend over and then stand up straight. But if one muscle contracts only partially or doesn't fully relax, the bones cannot return to their proper positions. The body does allow for temporary variations in contraction-relaxation to account for different situations, but over time it will "forget" its full alignment and balance.

Arguably, the musculoskeletal system has far more direct external interaction than other internal systems, which are tucked away deep inside the body's protective envelope. Your left ventricle doesn't stub its valves on rocks or bang up its knees playing basketball. Only skin has more exposure to earth, water, wind, and fire. It alone suffers from insect bites, poison ivy, and razor burn, not to mention more severe injuries. Our world is a rough place of many extremes; the sheer number of plausible ways to live, work, and play is huge. While the skin and other organs go along for the ride, the musculoskeletal system *is* the ride. We move it, and it moves us until we die.

Consequently, there is a wide range of performance—and that can be misleading. Mary is tall and thin, walks with a slight limp on the right side, and is an okay weekend ice skater but tires easily. Joe, short and fat, can't swivel his head more than a few degrees in either direction, spends much of his day at a desk or sitting in front of the TV at night, and has insomnia. Meanwhile, Sharon, an Olympic athlete, breaks records using the exact same musculoskeletal equipment (the same, that is, in terms of design function). For both Mary and Joe, their musculoskeletal systems, measured by miles traveled, loads lifted, and the daily routine of stretching, bending, twisting, turning, and artfully using their hands and feet, is a remarkable display of endurance and physical prowess, although it falls far short of Sharon's potential. Such wide disparity is typical—most people are more like Mary and Joe than Sharon—and it contributes to the false notion that the musculoskeletal system is, in general, an inferior piece of work, frail, accident-prone, and inconsistent.

Aspiring anatomical architects and engineers fancy that they can devise a better spine, a stronger knee, a longer-lasting hip. But the body is truly ingenious and already knows how to give reliable structure and coherent, multidirectional movement to 206 or so skeletal bones. Just being able to stand up, bear our own weight, and remain in place is a remarkable achievement. Walking is a miracle of coordination! No matter how it happened, we are lucky that our ancestors got an apparatus that allowed them and us to counteract gravity, to stand upright on two feet, and to smoothly walk and run from point A to point B—because we'd never be able to invent it from scratch on our own. Today's prosthetic devices are impressive in that they restore functions to people who have lost them. But, as anyone who wears a prosthesis can tell you, they are only rough approximations of the original limbs they replace.

Just in Case

As I explained in my book *Pain Free*, the design of the musculoskeletal system allows for temporary misalignment in case of accidents or unusual, life-or-death conditions when the system is under stress, yet this is meant to last for only a short time. Many people subject themselves to a nearly permanent state of misalignment that often lasts years. Something has to give, and it usually does.

Pain, limitation, and other problems aren't caused by the design and quality of the musculoskeletal system so much as the way we are using and misusing it and its component parts. Our upright, balanced, bipedal posture is a product of the messy, improvisatory business of climbing down from trees, getting our heads up over tall grasses, and getting our forepaws off the ground to hold weapons, tools, and food supplies. Until these changes occurred, our distant ancestors were little more than a bunch of hapless primates, the favorite lunchmeat of carnivores no bigger than French poodles. Thankfully for us, humankind stood up on two legs, started moving, and hasn't stopped since.

Going vertical required skeletal alignment, flexible and resilient jointure, close muscular coordination and orchestration, and a means of staying upright. Voilà! A two-legged, antigravity machine—an all-weather, all-terrain sport utility vehicle emerged from the mists of time. It is obvious that simple skeletal misalignment drastically impedes the function of the musculoskeletal system. Today, millions of people are slowly collapsing out of vertical alignment and losing their battle with gravity thanks to a sedentary lifestyle. They don't even get the minimal levels of motion required to maintain adequate muscle strength and engagement to support spinal function, skeletal alignment, balance, and proper joint interaction and articulation.

The Egoscue Method was devised to restore alignment by reintroducing motion that strengthens and re-engages temporarily dysfunctional supporting muscles and other musculoskeletal components. I call it *postural therapy*, a way to address injury and chronic pain without resorting to toxic drugs or invasive surgical procedures. Also, it is an effective technique for achieving peak athletic conditioning.

Or so I thought. Actually, I was correct, but my reasoning was wrong. I concluded that postural therapy is effective because misalignment is bad, and that proper skeletal alignment is good. From a literal and superficial standpoint, that's true.

Let's circle back to the exercise I asked you to do in Chapter 2. The primary purpose of the musculoskeletal system—*numero uno*—is to download and circulate high-wavelength energy to fuel the sixty trillion cells in the typical adult body. All the body's internal systems function more powerfully because adequate energy resources are available and, in turn, that enhanced function leads to the uptake of more energy, more capacity, and an increasingly healthy life. While the musculoskeletal system moves us, it also fuels us.

What's more, a strong, properly aligned and engaged musculoskeletal system makes it possible for your body's internal sensory apparatus to precisely monitor and choreograph the complex interplay of the chemical, electrical, biomechanical, and cellular processes. Simply by standing up on two feet—an overt act not unlike tuning an antenna—the body is informed within fractions of seconds to how well the liver is functioning and whether the heart is straining. Messages by the billions streak up the spine to the brain and orders race back down: sample, adjust, tweak, recalibrate, sample again. . . .

Musculoskeletal system misalignment, visible and measurable, is a reliable indicator of the body's inability to take on energy supplies. A misaligned musculoskeletal system triggers a host of warnings that activate hormonal responses that affect your mood, respiration, blood pressure, energy levels, and resistance to illness.

Not only does misalignment interfere with the flow of message traffic, it sends messages of its own announcing that the body is literally losing its life. Stiffness and immobility are two characteristics of a corpse. By cutting off oxygen, freezing joints, and contracting muscles, the musculoskeletal system concedes that gravity is winning, and *will* win.

★   ★   ★   ★   ★

Now I'm going to get a little technical—just a little. It is as if we have two metabolic loops, one for processing and utilizing energy derived from edible matter, and another for ingesting and digesting high-wavelength energy that radiates through the space we inhabit. Without the second high-wavelength energy loop, the first metabolic loop is under siege, struggling to keep the various internal systems efficient and healthy but losing ground over time. By firing up both loops simultaneously there is plenty of energy. The musculoskeletal system not only provides routine locomotion, it tells us directly, unmistakably, whether our energy intake is high or low.

Your car has a fuel gauge even though it will be obvious—and inconvenient—when the tank runs dry. The human body has one as well. Instead of a little arrow pointing at the half mark, your shoulders and spine do the pointing by rounding and slumping; you lose skeletal alignment, and with it, balance is also lost. As the head begins to hang forward and down (and other musculoskeletal components lose their verticality), the arrow goes to the quarter mark or less. As a result, major posture muscles are losing even more of their energy charge as tone, length, and strength dwindle.

The musculoskeletal system plainly displays, in real time, how much or how little energy is on board. I suspect that our earliest ancestors chose mates, hunting partners, and leaders by intuitively making alliances with those who *looked right*. They read the body language, the posture, and correlated it to the likelihood of success based on the appearance of those who had succeeded in the past. An upright, balanced posture was empirical evidence of strength, stamina, and prehistoric street smarts.

Today, your posture is capable of sending the same positive message or delivering a dire warning. I believe you are capable of reading those warnings; you've got all the right equipment, and that is why I'm going to keep yammering at you about the importance of musculoskeletal balance.

Balance, balance, and more balance . . . you either have it or you are losing your perfect health.

SIX

BALANCE OF FORCES

FROM THE VERY FIRST DAYS OF HUMAN HISTORY, success and failure, perfect health and serious illness, happiness and despair have had distinct postures. We wear our health like a cloak.

Just as a modern sailor knows how to interpret subtle changes in wind direction, currents, and cloud cover to predict weather patterns (they'll tell you they can *feel* that the weather is about to change), Neolithic warrior chiefs and Roman generals could forecast the impending victory or defeat of their armies by watching the way the infantry marched into battle.

Those commanders carefully inspected their troops. They noted an uncertain gait, restricted arm swing, or labored pace, and accurately foresaw disaster ahead. Or perhaps they observed heads held high, squared shoulders, self-confidence, boundless energy, and the fierce joy that presages triumph. Pure *WYSIWYG*: what you see is what you get. Yet those leaders would probably have scoffed at the idea that they could read the army's combined musculoskeletal arsenal the same way they could inspect and evaluate a battery of catapults or a squadron of cavalry. Rather, it was a regarded as a hunch, an intuition, a gut check, or maybe even a magic trick. Actually, they were tapping into a special human resource—feelings drawn from a deep pool of emotions linked to an even deeper reservoir of collective experience.

The solitary soldier felt it too and also knew the meaning of what he felt.

Today, the posture you see continues to be what you get—and is derived from what you feel. But many of us have been persuaded to distrust and ignore the feelings conveyed by our posture. Instead of listening to those messengers and taking heed, we try to silence them with powerful drugs, invasive medical procedures, and the opinions of others—a huge irony, since many of us are certainly descendants of men and women who were acutely aware of their own feelings, acted on them, and lived to fight another day (and pass on their genes).

Did they at least suspect that what they saw and felt was the result of musculoskeletal system balance or the lack of it? I doubt it. The body informs; it doesn't explain. Explanations are the work of the thinking mind rather than the aware mind. Does this stimulus feel good or bad? Is it enjoyable or not? Our ancestors used their aware mind to choose the ways and means to sustain positive feelings that were being generated, or, if the feelings were negative, to avoid as best they could whatever it was that was producing bad feelings. The truth doesn't need an explanation or expert validation; instead, it must feel right.

Never Mind

Have you lost your mind? Don't bother looking under the chair. You never had one. The brain actually exists as corporel matter. A surgeon can open the skull of a living human and examine brain tissue. There is no mind, however. It's been described—ludicrously, I believe—as an immaterial substance. A what? The mind is more usefully understood as a process of the brain for recording and organizing experience. The mind is, in effect, a faulty memory. Faulty because it leaks its contents—memories, lingering displacement patterns of energy waves associated with past events—into our consciousness instead of keeping them sealed away in the background.

The memory, as repository of non-extant stimulus, seems to be walled off from the present in other creatures; nonetheless, it informs and helps shape present actions. For instance, a hungry seagull learns that hanging out at the town dump is an easy way to get food, but the bird doesn't consciously think about the connection, much less deliberately assign value. The stomach rumbles and wings flap to the nearest landfill. This scruffy gourmand learns to repeat a past action over and over again, but doesn't reason. That last step—reasoning—happens only to creatures with leaky memories who have reasoned themselves into possession of a "mind" and spent the better part of a hundred thousand years developing that faculty by reliving the past and trying to control the future.

Indeed, *what you see is what you get* is true. And *what you feel is what you get* is even truer. Posture is the mechanism that guides human beings to this essential fact. Balance feels good; imbalance feels bad. Without balance you cannot access your aware mind; all emotions except fear are walled off, out of reach. But protracted periods of full-blown fear were relatively uncommon (see Chapter 4) until recently. Pleasure was a more familiar emotion, as was its linkage to success and self-confidence.

The human body is extremely sensitive to imbalance because it can only be caused by lack of adequate high-wavelength energy. Our ancestors didn't know high-wavelength energy from Zeus' thunderbolts, but when those marching Roman legionnaires were balanced, they consequently felt invincible. They had the inner resources—strength, stamina, and willpower—to conquer the world. Out of balance, they felt vulnerable, and they were.

By rediscovering the primary purpose of musculoskeletal system balance and achieving that balance, you are in a position to reclaim an important health legacy:

Peace of mind.

Hold on; don't write off peace of mind as a hippy-dippy, space cadet state of goofy detachment. Peace of mind is the pillar that supports courage, wisdom, and happiness.

The exercise that you did in Chapter 2 demonstrates that peace of mind awaits your summons. When you plug into the universal power grid by balancing your posture and drawing on its high-wavelength energy, the mental and physical static quiets down; in its place are clarity and focus. The incoming energy flow smooths turbulence by augmenting and supporting the metabolic power required to renew the body's cells. That same power is needed to fuel cells and build, maintain, and operate your many systems. This infusion of high-wavelength energy serves to remove waste, fight disease, and allow you, in general, to kick back and enjoy life's pleasures. You are able to live in the present where the aware mind connects to feelings that accurately convey what the body needs to remain optimally healthy.

You experienced a small taste of that in Chapter 2 by briefly trying a posture-balancing exercise. If you used proper form, you may have felt the following:

- Your weight was equally balanced on both feet side to side and front to back.
- Your load-bearing joints (ankles, knees, shoulders, and hips) were vertically aligned.
- Those joints, arranged in pairs, were also aligned horizontally on parallel planar surfaces side to side.
- There was an S-curve in the spine that held the upper torso upright.
- Shoulders were back over the hips and aligned as a pair on each side.

- The head was level, riding on your neck (the top of the spine) in vertical alignment over the pelvis.
- Imaginary lines drawn through these musculoskeletal components formed ninety-degree angles and a stable but flexible, ladder-like structure.

If someone had snapped a picture of you at the time you were doing the exercise, you would have seemed younger, stronger, healthier, and happier.

All About Balance

Postural balance looks good —because it is good. We like the look of it because we value the feel of it even more. Far more than the comeliness or athletic talent that some people have and others lack, balance perfectly equips each individual to move freely while at the same time guarding his or her own health. Balance is not optional. Without balance, those who believe the human body cannot cope with the demands of modern life are correct. There is no substitute for postural balance.

One look at our friends Mary and Joe from Chapter 5 tells me all I need to know. They are out of balance and, consequently, badly lack energy. Their postures do not reflect age, accidents, heredity, disease, or bad habits. Diet, weekly trips to the gym, joint replacement, or exotic pharmaceutical concoctions won't offer much lasting help. The best remedy for what ails Mary and Joe is the courage to make independent decisions based on how they *feel* about their health. Courage requires energy—a lot of energy. By returning to postural balance, they'll top off their depleted energy supplies, obtain the inner resources to make corrective changes, and put an end to years of being unaware of what their bodies have been trying to tell them. They'll have peace of mind. And in the event that those "important things" include warnings of serious illness brought on by their long-term energy deficits—which the body is hard-wired to detect—Mary and Joe will be aware of them and aware of what has to be done.

By returning to musculoskeletal system balance, they can access the flow of limitless energy that brings peace of mind, lack of fear, and strength to heal. Without balance, all of us are left in double jeopardy. We lack the high-wavelength energy to sustain our health, and don't have the assurance—let's hear it for national health assurance—that our bodies give us reliable feedback on whether our actions (lifestyle, choices, habits, and so on) are helping or hurting. Humans have a subtle yet immensely powerful emotional apparatus assigned to perform those missions. To be cut off from it is a sad fate for creatures that have clocked more than a million years by relying on the emotional *feel* of things rather than the *think* of things (to borrow a phrase attributed to Stanley Kubrick, the great film director).

I do not see it as a choice between modern medical care and faith healing. Yes, faith is involved—faith in yourself, faith in your innate ability to act in your own best interest. Yet, faith does not preclude using technology or expertise as long as your emotional radar is switched on. As complicated as medical treatment has become, you can still keep faith with the body's unerring wisdom, but only if you regain and maintain balance and listen to its messages.

Still have doubts about the essential role of postural balance? I'm not surprised. Don't take my word for it—words rely too heavily on the think of things. Get the feel of it for yourself, and then you'll be ready to live well and do it with peace of mind.

SEVEN

HALO . . . HALO . . .

I WOULD LIKE TO INTRODUCE YOU to another feeling. This one is generated by an exercise similar to the one I asked you to do in Chapter 2, only it is a little more dramatic. I am assuming—and believe me, it is a safe assumption—that you are way out of balance and running low on positive, high-wavelength energy. If not, good on you, as my Aussie friends say, but a brief refresher course won't hurt at all. The demonstration of Attractor energy can be underwhelming to some people because their energy resources are so depleted. The small spurt of energy that is generated by using positive words as opposed to negative words can be difficult for them to detect.

With this exercise, you can raise the intensity of the feeling and at the same time produce a sensation that for most people is unambiguously beneficial. In other words, I think you're going to like it.

Stand naturally, for example, like you normally do. Don't square up or try to balance yourself. I want you to be initially in an unbalanced state. Okay, look around the room you are in. Spot something that you don't like: a crooked picture frame, a pile of newspapers, a cluttered shelf. There is usually something that's less than perfect. Your thinking mind is a critic; you'll find something not to like.

Stare at the mess, and let it sink in. Tune in to how it makes you feel—angry at yourself for not cleaning up; exasperated;

determined to fix things; surprised. One Egoscue Method client did this exercise over the phone from his office and experienced a slight feeling of breathlessness when he noticed his supply closet was a slum. He was ashamed. You should definitely have a reaction to what seems like confirmation that you are not in complete control of your environment.

Close your eyes for about a minute and then open them again. The same mess across the room hasn't moved.

Now close your eyes and square up: head, neck, and shoulders back; feet hips-width apart; and weight balanced evenly on the ball of each foot. Take a few deep breaths and exhale. Stay there for about a minute and then open your eyes.

Behold the trouble spot. What does it feel like now? Focus. Give it a moment. Has that original reaction from the unbalanced position changed? Is there new information reaching you?

Many people immediately sense that the mess, the trouble spot, has become far less important. The urgency is gone, the pressure is off. The flaking paint on the ceiling can wait . . . the supply closet is fine. They are getting a flow of high-wavelength energy that is telling them, "This is no big deal. Relax."

Let's try something else. Sit down and take a short break. I want you to lapse back into an unbalanced state. Stand up and keep your posture natural. No cheating; you don't usually stand with your shoulders pulled back like that. Let them roll forward.

Everyone has a sense of their personal space. Can you estimate yours? Where does your personal space, that small zone that you prefer to keep clear of intruders, begin? One foot out? Two or three? When a stranger approaches too closely and you become uncomfortable, he has invaded your personal space. Estimate the size of that zone and close your eyes. Go through all the squaring and balancing-up procedures we used earlier. Don't forget your feet—parallel and straight ahead, hips-width apart. Balance your weight equally side to side and front to back. Hold the posture for two minutes.

Open your eyes. How far out does the personal space extend now?

Yeah, it's increased, perhaps by three or four feet.

You have an aura, an energy field that radiates out from your body much like the halos on saints depicted by fourteenth-century Italian painters. Perhaps Saint Francis of Assisi actually walked around with his hair on fire, but I tend to doubt it. More likely, artists could feel the saint's energy and were moved to give it a concrete expression in the form of a halo.

As you lose balance and energy, your aura shrinks. There's certainly not enough to light up a halo, and personal space no longer demarks a zone under your control but one that has been breached and cannot supply a sense of security. A "distant," "cold," and "guarded" person is struggling to protect herself from the loss of her aura by throwing up a wide defensive perimeter. Before, she became anxious when people came within a foot or two. Now, as her aura drains away, being in the same room with a stranger is troubling. The overriding impulse is to run and hide.

A Closer Look at Action and Optimism

For the purposes of our discussion, let's define energy as the capacity for action. The human body is a highly organized system with a truly impressive capacity and wide range for taking action in at least three forms: rote, repetitive action; innovative, first-of-its-kind action that arises in response to a new experience; and involuntary action without conscious volition, such as a heartbeat. In other words, to address the first and second of the three categories, we can remember how we moved an hour ago and duplicate that action if need be, or act in new and different ways without prior experience or preprogramming. The important point is that sudden, unexpected changes in circumstances that require innovative action are not major challenges. Witness human history and the unprecedented actions recorded in everything from arts to sports. Our innovative action generates a distinct attitude or mood that has come to be known as an optimistic outlook. Through a working partnership of (1) the physical functions that directly carry out innovative acts and (2) the mind that accepts the innovative requirement emotionally while supporting it cognitively, this optimism leads us to intuitively understand and embrace change as a beneficial process.

Optimism seeks the long view; it regards the unavoidable events of life—pain, rejection, disappointments—not as insurmountable obstacles or distressing symptoms to be treated in crisis mode but as part of the natural process of change. "Taking things in stride" is an optimistic life view. This attitude exists only as long as the individual retains full capacity for action; that is, absolute emotional certainty that he has the inner resources to successfully manage change without abject fear of failure.

The lower the external energy frequency, the less capable we become moment to moment, day to day, week to week. Pessimism replaces optimism.

There is no pill you can take to restore a lost aura, although many medications attempt to simulate a response that superficially resembles a charged-up energy field: sleeplessness, high blood pressure, rapid heartbeat, jumpiness, impulsive behavior (or its polar opposite, indecision), and the like. Medical researchers keep looking for ways to replace the "broken" part that produces the aura or other "lost" physiological functions.

Broken? Lost? Not!

EIGHT

STORYTELLERS

"SING TO ME OF THE MAN, MUSE, the man of twists and turns. . . ."

As one who stands in awe of the human musculoskeletal system with its splendid carrying capacity for heroism and folly, I reread Robert Fagles' translation of the first line of the *Odyssey* and it always stuns me.

Before pausing for breath, Homer casts a magic spell to conjure up a "man of twists and turns . . . ," deftly capturing our legacy of muscle and movement.

Odysseus—the man of twists and turns—is the first Everyman of literature, not counting Enkidu, a character in the four-thousand-year-old *Epic of Gilgamesh*. This poem, carved on stone tablets and buried in a Middle Eastern desert, was discovered a century ago. Enkidu has his fans, yet as a proxy or double for the Babylonian warrior god Gilgamesh, he rode on supernatural coattails—not fair!—and therefore lost stature.

Fiction, whether it is epic verse or modern potboiler, is a form of biography, an account of events and adventures that take place as the quest for life's meaning unfolds. Odysseus and Enkidu discover that nothing is permanent, everything keeps changing.

The realization comes as a great shock to both fictional characters and real people. Modern storytellers still grapple with the implications. All living things are in permanent negotiations with their environment over what must be done to accommodate change.

Each of us creates a story that explains who we are and why we are. Like Homer, we commit it to memory (not paper, not even granite tablets) and thereby imbue the story with transcendent power. Shakespeare's *Hamlet* begins with the question that launches all stories: "Who's there?" Nearly four hours later the suspects have been rounded up—adulterers, murderers, lunatics, the heartbroken, vengeance seekers, the unlucky, and all the rest is silence.

Without exception, visitors to an Egoscue Method clinic bring a story with them. I suspect that is also true for every other alternative and mainstream health-care operation in the world. People never leave home without their story.

Over the years, I have learned to listen closely to those stories, and I have discovered just how important they are. The narratives can be filled with insightful information, plot points, character development, surprises, growth, confusion, crisis, and suspense. Many physicians and other health practitioners think they don't have time for these stories. They speed-listen for ten minutes, home in on the usual symptomatic patterns, order up a few tests, and diagnose. Their Newtonian micro-medicine—the quest to find the broken part, no matter how small it is—rules out other options, even though modern medicine tends to treat the symptoms and not the problem anyway.

In the process, there is a huge disconnect. The physician is unable to make more than a cursory use of an invaluable resource, and the patient cannot determine whether the person he or she has turned to for help fully understands their situation. The uncertainty can cast a dark shadow over the relationship at the precise moment it needs to be on the firmest possible footing.

So, it is another example of bad doctors and good patients who are poorly served, right? No, not really.

The fault lies with the stories. Severe musculoskeletal system imbalance and the resulting acute energy shortage have frightened people facing unwelcome, unavoidable change, doubt, complexity, and mystery. Stories that once were told to provide hope, strength, and patience now spark dread and helplessness in the storyteller. In short, our stories have little in common with Odysseus', which gave him the strength to find his way home—through twenty years of twists and turns, through bravery, trickery, and bloodshed.

Another important point about these stories: they are irrelevant. Change quickly washes away context. For example, a valid observation about your health or mental outlook that a doctor made six months ago, let alone six years ago, has lost all but the slightest shadow of its original meaning. Change is so pervasive—from the external stimulus of a changing environment to the inner landscape that results from the body's response. Stories are generally woven together using incidents, episodes, and individual crises to form an overview. The product is then used to explain the past. In the hands of someone with a negative mind-set, this overview becomes an encyclopedia of excuses—an autobiography of failure. Worse, this method of storytelling is held up as an indispensable way to prepare for the future and manage outcomes. Stories such as these are in the same league as the utterances of false prophets.

A ten-year-old story is worthless. The client who brings it to us is not the same person as he was when it happened. But he may try to be, thereby creating havoc through poor choices, frustration, and anger.

For roughly my first twenty years as a postural therapist, I considered the stories my clients brought with them on their initial visits to the clinic to be, at best, a package of clues that explained why they were in pain or, at worst, a social nicety that allowed us to build a solid working relationship. I hardly noticed the obvious: the clients who made the most progress on correcting their musculoskeletal dysfunctions were the ones who readily put their stories aside. They focused on how they were feeling at that moment, not on the memory of how it felt when they were told at age fourteen that they had scoliosis or other chronic conditions. As

I encouraged them to change their posture and range of motion, they felt the pain diminish and function return. The old story ceased to matter as a new autobiography took shape.

I concluded that it was best to get the storytelling over the sooner the better, and to encourage the client to pay attention to how he or she feels—not how they felt. That protocol worked, except for a small percentage of people who used their stories to explain why they couldn't possibly get well. Frustrated, I would often—way too often—shoot holes in their story to force them to give it up.

As long as the numbers were small, I could persuade myself that the Egoscue Method was amazingly effective. We are now up to close to a million people who have been helped by the method. The failure rate for many years was about 3 percent. Statistically speaking, that's pretty good. But the thought that I couldn't help some three thousand people really bothered me. Even more disturbing, the failure rate began moving higher as musculoskeletal imbalance became the new normal.

After much soul searching, I decided that the only solution was to devise a way for the client to change his or her story without being forced to admit that he was changing it. Reworking the heath-care paradigm one story at a time was extremely daunting until I realized that all the problematic stories were fear-based. Furthermore, each fit into one of three broad variations that can be deconstructed like this:

- I've been to everyone and tried everything. Nothing works. I don't know where to turn. Help me if you can, but you probably can't. This is not my fault.
- I'm determined to figure this out and to take control. What's your solution? There are so many moving parts. Your recommendations are in conflict with other schools of thought. Have you considered . . . ? I need another opinion. Are you aware of this new study?

- What makes you so smart? None of this stuff works. It's all a scam. Nobody has an answer. Prove it. I don't feel any different.

I hope that captures the emotional and behavioral predilections of the three without holding them up to ridicule or suggesting that one or another is more or less desirable. I do not want to offend you—because your story may fit one of these categories.

The storytellers behind all three of these variations are afraid to go inward to obtain and marshal the resources needed to recover or sustain their own health. The stories were self-created to shield them from fear and to allow them to go on living in the presence of it. The storytellers inadvertently walled themselves off by denying personal responsibility, insatiably seeking new facts and treatment options without making commitments, or unintentionally wrapping themselves in the Teflon of cynicism to stand aloof on the sidelines.

Your own story is much richer, deeper, and meatier than my abbreviated outline, but if you can feel your way to the essence of the story I believe you will find a platform from which, together, you and I can work to restore your postural balance, your limitless energy, and your perfect health.

In the next three chapters I will describe the musculoskeletal markers of the three story lines and personality types. There are physical and functional characteristics for each. You'll be able to pick them out of a crowd; better yet, you'll be able to look in the mirror and recognize yourself. Then I will present menus of E-cises (Egoscue exercises) that can help recover musculoskeletal system balance and which are tailored to work with your specific story and type.

Rather than falling back on your story to explain why you can't restore your balance—*I'm too busy, it's too late, it runs in the family, it's a birth defect, Egoscue's too pushy*—focus on how you can really do this.

Really.

You are enough.

NINE

BLAME BLAM

NEVER EXPLAIN, NEVER COMPLAIN is a pretty good rule, yet I'm going to break half of it. I'm not a complainer, but when I blow it, the least I can do is give you a heads-up about what went wrong and why.

In my first book, *The Egoscue Method of Health Through Motion*, I described the outward physical characteristics of three categories of musculoskeletal system dysfunction, and offered guidance on how readers could easily figure out whether they fit into Conditions I, II, or III. The idea was to provide a process for self-diagnosis that would set the stage for the next step: do-it-yourself postural therapy that addressed the specifics of each condition. As I wrote at the time, when you know what to look for, musculoskeletal misalignment and imbalance are easy to spot.

Strike Three

What surprised me, however, was that many people couldn't do it. In particular, readers whose posture was most similar to Condition III were entirely confused by the drawings and written description. Only the most intrepid readers could bring themselves to gaze into the mirror and admit they looked that bad. Condition II's were slightly better at self-diagnosis, but not by much.

Both Condition IIs and Condition IIIs, even if they were in horrible pain, tended to choose Condition I, which led them to follow an E-cise menu that didn't work as well.

Amazingly, I still get rave reviews for the book. People call the Del Mar clinic out of the blue to tell me how good those E-cises make them feel. When I ask a few questions about what's currently going on with their body and hear answers that indicate that they are classic, industrial-strength Condition IIIs, I've learned to say, "Go to the E-cises for Condition III. Don't look at the pictures or read the description; just try the E-cise menu." Often they sound shocked that I would even think of linking them to Condition III. I fear that some of them put down the phone and, convinced they or I misunderstood, go straight back to Condition I. There's no harm done (on the contrary, a lot of help is delivered regardless of which menu is used), but they are not getting the full benefit of the method.

The sad truth is that today, more than ever, my unvarnished description of Condition III in *The Egoscue Method* is what most Americans and most affluent and middle-class people around the world look like and hurt like. Tragically, that look of imbalance and musculoskeletal misalignment has become the new normal. When the old normal walks by—a rarer and rarer occurrence—he or she seems strange.

Easy Rider

The individual vertebrae of the spine ride on cushions—spongy disks that resemble jelly donuts—that act as shock absorbers. Imbalance and misalignment result in the weight of the upper torso and head squeezing down on the disks unevenly to cause the "jelly" to either bulge from between the vertebrae or rupture (it actually pops like a balloon and the filling oozes out). Either way, the result is a painful nerve impingement.

Yet, even though this new normal has taken hold, there are still three broad categories of readily observable musculoskeletal system conditions. They are accompanied by overt behavioral patterns that are expressed as actions, attitudes, and emotions. I call them "AAE patterns."

To put it more plainly, it is not just the postures that matter—it's your head. To help you make a self-diagnosis, I don't have to show you any examples of dysfunction. Hallelujah! There's no need to scare you with lurid depictions of desperate people who are about to crash and burn. Instead, I will help you feel what's going on in your head, in your heart, and in your body's core systems that monitor and operate this amazing thing that we so casually refer to as human health. Best of all, you won't have to take my word for it. You know more about your body than any expert, because you feel it and they don't.

I started this book by asking, "How do you feel?" However, some people—perhaps you—can't answer that question because one of the three most common AAE patterns is disrupting their ability to get an accurate reading from their emotional feedback loop.

Example: J.B.'s back was hurting when he came to see me a couple of years ago at the San Diego clinic. He told me right off, "I've got a herniated disk."

Okay. That is not a nice thing to have. I asked him to stand pigeon-toed with both cheeks of the buttocks and his lower and upper back against the wall. Try it yourself: level your chin and make sure the back of your head is against the wall, otherwise there is a tendency for the head and neck to come forward and down. Now put your shoulders against the wall.

"How's it feel now?"

"Still hurts."

"Really?"

"Yeah, really. I can show you the X-ray of the disk."

"But it still hurts? No change?"

"Of course."

Making Choices

Instead of starting with a demonstration of how postural balance can switch off the pain symptom, we have a discussion of whether the client wants a cure or treatment. Surprisingly, about one in twenty clients say they want treatment.

I didn't argue with J.B., but I knew that the pigeon-toed stance temporarily repositioned his hips and in so doing moved the affected vertebrae off the distended disk to free the jammed nerve. Without the impingement, the magnitude of the pain had to decrease. While there might have been an echo of tenderness, the worst of the pain went away almost immediately. J.B.'s reaction didn't surprise me, though. His feelings were being distorted by his default AAE pattern. He was a big, strong, courageous guy, yet fear and a history of pain had switched off his ability to accurately assess what was going on in his back.

Pain is not a disease, not an injury, not even an effect of aging. Pain is a symptom—in J.B.'s case, a symptom of postural imbalance. Not the only one; there were many others that produced little or no pain at all. The way he sliced a golf ball, for instance (pain free as long as you weren't in the line of fire), and the contortions he went through to get in and out of his car—J.B. drove a low-slung Italian job, and he struggled to lower himself into the driver's seat—

caused serious pain. Eventually, he sold it and bought something more sedate. But even his new luxury sedan was a challenge to J.B. until he got his functional posture back.

Symptoms are irrelevant—go for a cure. Cures come about only when the bullet of intervention is aimed at, and hits, the actual cause of a condition. Shooting innocent bystanders usually serves only to create collateral damage and costly medical bills.

Got Your Back

Favorite symptomatic treatments of herniated disks include removing the disk in conjunction with fusing the adjoining vertebrae, or trimming away the ruptured disk material. No matter what, the spine is still unbalanced and unevenly squeezing the remaining disks. Fusing the vertebrae worsens the imbalance and creates stress on the shoulders, hips, knees, and ankles, and snipping off the protruding disk material probably means you'll be having a lot of recurring back surgery.

For J.B., the cause of his condition was lack of energy. His back pain and postural imbalances were symptoms of an energy deficit that always occurs when the body is left unplugged. Just as the ice cream stored in your kitchen freezer will melt if the electricity goes out for a couple of hours, when the body goes off-line and loses contact with the universal power grid, it too melts. Musculoskeletal form and function are quickly lost without a constant flow of high-wavelength energy. Why? Death dematerializes living tissue. Only the subatomic structures endure forever. Short of death, the early, obvious, and progressive stages of dematerialization are the body's means of warning us that something is happening that in many cases—far more than we think— is within our power to substantially affect. By ignoring the message or merely addressing pain symptoms with painkillers, joint replacement, and other forms of surgery (treatment), the most important message of all is lost.

This is one of the most important points in the book. Your musculoskeletal system is the tripwire that sets off the first of many alarms. When our earliest ancestors first showed up on dry land, they didn't have the technological tools to explore inside the body, surf the bloodstream, test-drive the immune system, and the like. Instead, they relied on a simple awareness of seemingly superficial changes taking place on the body's surface or close to it: *My left foot is turned out instead of pointing straight ahead; my spear-chucking arm seems stiff; or I'm having trouble keeping pace with my favorite hunting companions.* Those folks weren't rocket scientists, yet they were smart enough to recognize that something had changed. Nothing comes of nothing. They learned to either alter the stimulus that was causing the change (finding a dry place to sleep in monsoon season, for instance), or they lived with the consequences, which often meant dying sooner rather than later. Natural selection favored those who took action based on awareness, and their biological heirs are still blessed with the tripwire provided by the musculoskeletal system.

J.B. has come a long way, but he has misplaced his awareness. If I could have waved a magic wand to instantly restore J.B.'s postural balance, his energy levels would have quickly topped off. What prevented that—aside from my wand being in the repair shop to have its abracadabra generator rebuilt—was that he was afraid to accept the idea that something as simple as postural balance was the answer. He resisted treatment in order to keep pursuing facts that he regarded as more plausible and reassuring.

J.B. found more comfort in seeking and collecting new facts, theories, information, and such that he got from living truly pain free. Fact collecting is a common AAE pattern (remember— *actions, attitudes, emotions*). J.B.'s body was aware of the dangerous shortage of energy and informed him of the situation with a variety of messages, including pain symptoms and such non-pain symptoms as fatigue, irritability, and lack of focus. But his thinking mind had outsmarted his feeling mind by persuading him that he could exert control over these symptoms by using his high IQ and practical experience. Like most fact collectors, however, the search for another set of new facts precludes fact-based actions. What's the point? The new new facts will blow away the old new facts. J.B. chased facts when all he had to do was stand there and feel the energy being renewed and his health restored as his body was temporarily brought back into balance.

I'll return to J.B. in a moment; meantime, I want to stop here briefly to deal more directly with the invisible elephant in the room: physical limitation, the werewolf of postural therapy. I've already discussed the importance of an individual's story. The story frames what would otherwise be a meaningless jumble of events, incidents, and sensations. The various pieces of a narrative give meaning and value to the life it represents. A story may be true or false, and in a general sense is neither good nor bad. It just is. Yet a story infused by forebodings of physical limitation and what they portend has the power to interfere with your feeling mind. As a creature of the night, it has sharp fangs and a hairy face.

J.B. saw the world as a dangerously complicated place. Consequently, he had to discover what makes it tick. He searched diligently for facts that would give him the ability to manage the present, predict and prepare for the future, and survive. It was a never-ending quest, because new facts are constantly trumping old facts. As a result, he never needed to make a choice and run the risk of being wrong, which in a complicated, dangerous world could be lethal. Hence, J.B.'s story is crippled by his compulsion to keep collecting facts.

The second of these AAE patterns is skepticism. Like fact collecting, skepticism is also driven by anxiety about physical limitation, which lodges in the emotional catacombs when the musculoskeletal system first experiences a gap in its repertoire of movement. L.J., a child psychologist, freely admitted she was skeptical of anyone and anything who claimed to be able to solve problems or accomplish objectives. She was always on guard against being conned. For her, everyone was a suspect with a hidden agenda. It was L.J.'s job to find it. Acute skepticism protected her from ever making an affirmative decision, and hence she was never responsible for her own problems, including her health.

The third AAE pattern is pessimism, the most extreme form of limitation dread. Tommy worked in pessimism the way some artists work in watercolors. He sought help from dozens of health-care practitioners and was always willing to try another therapeutic program, but believed that they would fail because he didn't deserve to succeed.

I am about to introduce three chapters that will offer more information on these behavioral patterns, including recommendations for postural therapy programs that have a demonstrated ability to overcome them. The catch is, I don't know which one of them is affecting you. It's going have to be your call, your decision.

I can't knock experts who are ready, willing, and able to assume responsibility for your health, but I am a complete exception to their rules. I concede that the road from here on belongs to you. Notice that I've avoided linking the patterns closely to an individual. It doesn't matter who you are, what you do, or if you are young, old, male, or female. Read all three of the following chapters and—by the feel of it, not the think of it—decide which of them may be affecting your ability to live pain free. Try the postural therapy program that is the best remedy for your specific fear pattern. Again, by the feel of it, not the think of it, decide if the program works. If not, reread the chapters (or the entire book) and try another program. You may need to try all three before you find the best one for you. Take your time; stay in the moment.

Just ask yourself—*How do I feel?*

TEN

THE WEIGHT OF
EVIDENCE

IN THE LAST CHAPTER I PROMISED to introduce you to the three personality types that are the most threatened by musculoskeletal system imbalance. Of the three personality types, fact collectors are my favorite. They require a steady supply of new facts, and usually they are quite easy to deliver as long we are careful to distinguish between external facts and internal facts.

The human musculoskeletal system is a symphony of facts, but as obsessed as they are with collecting them, fact collectors like J.B. (who was featured in the preceding chapter, so if you skipped over it you might want to backtrack a little) are conditioned to gather only facts from external sources that legitimize, sanction, and officially confirm that what the collector sees, smells, tastes, touches, and hears is the real deal. As a result, J.B. rarely looked within himself to discover and authenticate those facts. This is a problem, to say the least.

By establishing a higher authority to validate facts, J.B. disenfranchised himself. Humans have a gift for discerning the real from the unreal, truth from falsehood, the genuine from the fake. If we didn't, our species would have become extinct thousands of years ago. There's far too much quicksand, thin ice, slipperiness in the dark, and dangerous places and creatures to not have a reasonably effective means for screening out the phony and the fallacious.

Thanks to your ancestors, who learned the hard way to live on and rule over this planet, you are nobody's fool. Before there was a thinking mind, there was—and still is—an aware mind that allows humans to quickly distinguish between things that are promising and those that are perilous. The aware mind accomplishes this by accessing subjective, road-tested standards imbedded deep in our sensory apparatus. Objective facts have little or no relevance to the aware mind, which is tuned to a different frequency. It doesn't give a damn about the think of things. Subjective facts rule. Gathered over the course of time like scar tissue, they are a potent distillation drawn from the raw ingredients of personal experiences. What drips out of the spigot is one-thousand-proof feeling.

Fact collectors have lost contact with the aware mind. To them, a fact must have a pedigree, a seal of approval; otherwise, it is an opinion of limited value. J.B. and his cohorts come to the Egoscue clinics with MRIs, X-rays, file folders stuffed full of medical records, and vocabularies bristling with Latinate jargon. I used to refuse to look at the material, preferring instead to directly observe the individual's posture. Just as a connoisseur of pre-Columbian pottery would be put off if I refused to admire her treasures, the fact collectors were affronted by my indifference toward their precious, authenticated facts. Now, after a good twenty or more years of being obtuse, I make a point of reviewing the records and agreeing that, *Yes, the X-ray shows the disk is ruptured* or, *No doubt about it, that knee is badly swollen.*

Story attempts to provide meaning. By shaping a narrative out of all the bits and pieces of existence—here's the beginning, the middle, and the end—storytellers try to create coherence out of confusion. J.B.'s story, the one that helps him make sense of his life and calms his fears, is built around a core belief that he can be safe (or safer) as long as he can put a wall of facts between himself and the predator that is stalking him. Predators in this case might not consist of grizzlies and tigers, but, rather, limitation, illness, pain, aging, and death. A fact collector believes that if he can assemble all of the "true" facts of his situation, a solution will emerge. In other words, his story is a classic *whodunit* with the fact collector starring as the heroic private eye.

Facts become all-important. People like J.B. shop for facts, savor facts, trade in dented and scratched old facts for bright, shiny new facts. It doesn't take long for fact finding to become a substitute for action. Instead of making a decision and following through on it to change the conditions that are causing or contributing to the pain or other symptoms, fact collectors seek different sets of facts that are obligingly generated by medical science, the pharmaceutical industry, and experts of every sort. They are free to choose a fact to their liking and use it as a basis for treatment or cure—and that's fine. However, most often it is an excuse to avoid treatment altogether, since a new fact is waiting just around the next corner. Fact collectors also possess a tendency to passively submit to someone else's opinion on what is best because that person is offering a convincing presentation of the facts—which might happen to coincide with a symptom that has become too painful or unpleasant to be endured.

My challenge as a postural therapist is to figure out a way to get the inner voice of the aware mind within earshot of a fact collector's inner facts. Once that happens, the need for another set of new, externally generated facts usually fades away. Feelings are better than facts. A balanced musculoskeletal system feels right (and it is!). By offering J.B. a few E-cises to stabilize his posture, I could then ask, "How does that feel?" and get a useful answer.

"It feels a little better."

"Good. You still have a ruptured disk—that's a fact."

"That's true."

"But these E-cises affected the pain—that also seems to be a fact, doesn't it?"

"Yeah."

"Does it make sense to you to continue the E-cises and see what happens?"

"Well, the E-cises do seem to work. My low back feels different."

Most fact collectors will go home from the clinic, think about their first visit, and come back with a couple of other facts. Maybe they've called their doctor or gone on the Internet. The Web is teeming with facts. I've learned not to argue with those external facts. The best approach is to return to the inner facts. "How do you feel?"

"A little better. But my left knee has started to hurt again."

"What's that tell you?"

"Maybe I'm standing up straighter, and the knee isn't used to that."

"If you are, we are impacting the dysfunction, jump-starting disused muscles. Let's see if we can build on this progress. Want to give it a shot?"

The Role of Energy Depletion

I don't have the slightest interest in being in the external-fact business. I'm inviting him to believe his inner facts and to link them to the gradually receding pain and other symptoms such as the knee. I used to think that postural balance—even partially restored balance—felt so good that clients would always feel compelled to respond immediately. But I now believe that when high-wavelength energy is depleted, it may take several tries to get it back to a level that is sufficient to completely switch off the craving for external facts. Awareness requires energy. When you can't go there, it usually means that your musculoskeletal system imbalance has drained your energy supply to

the extent that it is almost empty. Yet just by making a brief recon-
nect in the form of a simple balancing E-cise, energy starts flowing
again—a lot of energy.

Even so, a fact collector will be tempted to stop and carefully
scrutinize her vast fact collection, comparing the newcomers to the
old favorites. This can be frustrating. Instead of moving forward,
she digs in her heels, seeks to question everything, and arranges and
rearranges the facts in order to assign more value to some and less to
others. Hairs are split and angels dance on the heads of pins. It helps
to have an abundance of patience; otherwise, fact collectors start to
seem unreasonably rigid and prone to willfully obstructing a cure.

Indeed, rigidity is the overarching postural and emotional
characteristic of fact collectors. They are tight, stiff, tense,
constricted. The facts don't give them any wiggle room. Life isn't
much fun. When they look to the right or left they cannot just
move their head; their whole body rotates. If you had removed the
driver's-side mirror from his car before his cure, J.B. would have
been unable to glance over his shoulder at the traffic approaching
from the left rear. His peripheral vision was poor; when walking he
plodded along. There was very little spontaneity or variation in his
stride.

When he first came to the clinic and stood sideways next to
a ceiling-to-floor plumb-line, J.B.'s ankle was on the line but his
knee, hip, upper torso, shoulder, neck, and ear fell in front of it. He
thought he was standing straight, but he was actually raked forward
like the bow of a ship. The body's internal sensors read his posture
and concluded that he was only a few degrees away from toppling
forward. Red alert! J.B.'s muscles were contracted from his head
to his feet. His joints were locked tightly to hold his body upright,
sacrificing lateral movement and rotational flexibility in the interest
of keeping him from going horizontal.

Bear in mind that this is not routine posture for *anyone*. It is the
posture of crisis and calamity. Whenever a fact collector is on his feet,

the internal alarm bells are ringing big-time, the nervous system is fired up, and energy is being poured into vital physiological processes that for all they know are about to be asked to function in a state of emergency. And our guy is only walking from his easy chair to the bathroom! Ironically, most fact collectors aren't couch potatoes. They keep fairly active. I see them rigid and running, rigid and inline skating, rigid and golfing, and rigidly playing a variety of weekend sports—because the facts say they need to keep fit. They also frequently hurt themselves, at which point they start collecting facts to prove that running when you're over forty is hard on the knees, tennis rackets stress your elbow, and golf is hard on the back.

However, those are external facts. Restoring balance by just 10 or 15 percent delivers an instant energy payoff. By accumulating high-wavelength energy rather than running a deficit, even the most dedicated fact collector quickly starts to feel better. Once postural balance is restored, he loses the urgent compulsion to grab at external facts to explain his sense of panic and foreboding. His aware mind is re-invigorated. J.B. and others like him can live in the moment, drawing pleasure and peace of mind where he once hustled after facts to compensate for not being present.

Are you a fact collector? Before you answer, mull over the following questions:

- How do you make decisions? Fast or slow? Is it easy or do you agonize?
- Are you prone to second-guessing your decisions?
- Do you frequently change your mind?
- How do you rate yourself as a decision maker?
- Are you afraid of making mistakes?
- What was your best decision?
- What was your worst decision?
- Are you stubborn?
- Are you a perfectionist?

- Who is the smartest person you know?
- Do you welcome responsibility?
- Are you rigid?
- Do you go by the book?
- Are there decisions you prefer to avoid?

So? Or do you need more facts?
Here's one—balance. Try it. Please.

E-cise Menu for Fact Collectors

STATIC BACK

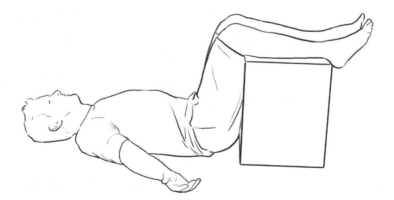

This E-cise uses the force of gravity to settle the hips, back, and shoulders to the floor and put them into a neutral position. Lie on your back with both legs bent at right angles and resting on a chair, a bench, or a block. Rest your hands on your stomach, or on the floor, below shoulder level, and with palms up. Let the back settle into the floor. Breathe from your diaphragm. That is, do stomach breathing—the abdominal muscles should rise as you inhale and fall as you exhale. Stay in this position for 10 minutes. Relax.

KNEE-PILLOW SQUEEZES IN STATIC BACK

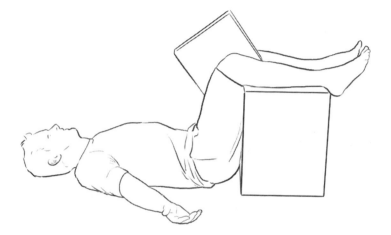

Stay in Static Back position. Widen your feet to allow a fat pillow or a foam block to fit between your knees. Squeeze the knees together using the inside (abductor) muscles of the thighs. Give the pillow a firm squeeze, then release. Don't tighten your abdominal muscles. Do 3 sets of 20 repetitions.

To learn more about the exercises in this chapter, please refer to the E-Cise Menu for Fact Collectors on the Pain Free Living *DVD.*

HIP LIFTS

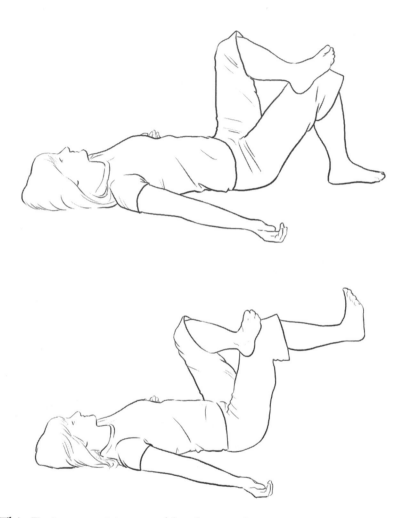

This E-cise repositions and levels your hips. Lie on your back with both knees bent and your feet flat on the floor. Cross your left ankle on your right knee, then press your left knee away from your body. While maintaining this position, lift your right foot off the floor, bringing both legs toward your chest. Make sure your hips stay squared and on the floor, that your left knee is still pressing out, and that your right leg is in line with your right shoulder. After 1 minute switch the legs and repeat on the other side.

HIP CROSSOVER

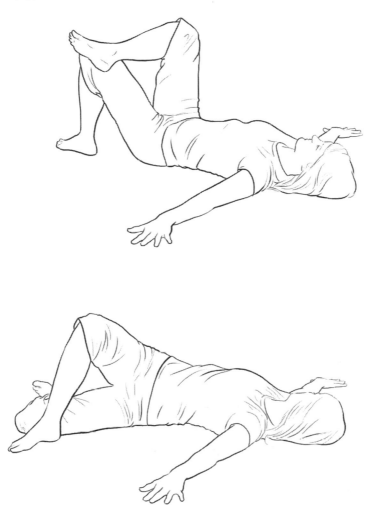

This E-cise counteracts hip rotation on both sides. Lie on your back with your knees bent and your feet flat on the floor. Place your arms flat on the floor at shoulder level. Cross your right ankle over your left knee, and rotate the ankle/knee combination to the floor to your left. Turn your head so that you are looking to the right, and relax your shoulders. Press your right knee away from your body with the right hip musculature. Switch the ankle/knee crossover, and repeat on the opposite side.

FROG

This E-cise positions the pelvis symmetrically left to right. Lie on your back with your knees bent. Make sure your feet are centered in the middle of your body, and let your knees and legs fall away to the sides. Put the soles of your feet together. Your low back does not need to be flat on the floor, and, in fact, there may be an arch due to the hips' changing position. Relax. Do not press the thighs out and down. Feel the stretch in the inner thighs and groin for 3 minutes.

STANDING ARM CIRCLES

This E-cise strengthens the muscles of the upper back that are involved with the shoulders' ball-and-socket function. Stand facing a full-length mirror with your feet parallel and toes pointing straight ahead. Place a pillow or inflatable block between your knees. Curl your fingertips into the pads of each palm (the fleshy area at the base of the fingers), and point your thumbs straight out. (This hand position, called the "golfer's grip," is imperative to the success of this E-cise.) Squeeze your shoulder blades together, and bring your arms out to the sides at shoulder level, elbows straight. With your palms facing down and thumbs pointed forward, circle up and forward. With your arms still out at shoulder level and palms up, circle up and back. Remember to keep your wrists, arms, and elbows straight, with the shoulder blades squeezed together. Don't contract your stomach muscles—the circles must come from the shoulders. Keep your neck and head back. Do 30 forward repetitions and 30 back repetitions.

STANDING QUAD STRETCH

Hip rotation shuts the quads off; this E-cise turns them back on. Stand on one foot and bend the other leg back, placing the top of the foot on a block or a chair seat. (The elevation should be somewhere between the bottom of the buttock and your hipline, and the amount of stretch depends on how high your foot is propped.) Keeping the hips and shoulders square and the knees even, tuck your hips under to feel the stretch. Hold on to something for balance. One side will probably be tighter than the other, but do not vary the foot elevation from side to side. Stretch for 1 minute for each leg.

CATS AND DOGS

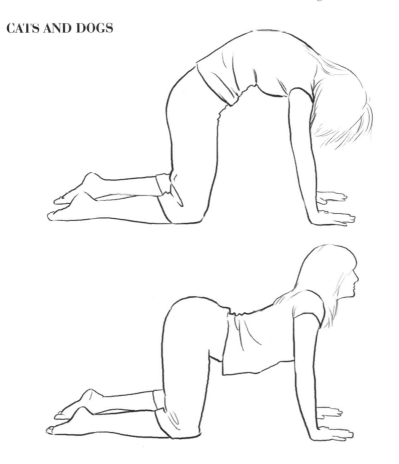

This E-cise works the hips, spine, shoulders, and neck in coordinated flexion-extension. Get down on the floor on your hands and knees, making sure that your knees are aligned with your hips, wrists, and shoulders, and that your lower legs are parallel with each other and with your hips. Make sure your weight is distributed evenly. Smoothly round your back as your head curls down to create a curve that runs from the buttocks to the neck—this is the cat with an arched back. Smoothly sway the back down while bringing the head up—this is the perky dog. Make these two moves flow continuously back and forth rather than allowing them to be distinct and choppy. Do 10 repetitions, with each cat-and-dog combo counting as a single rep.

ELEVEN

THE SKEPTIC AND THE GOSPEL OF DOUBT

Read any good autobiographies lately?

You have if you looked into the mirror today or glanced at a passing stranger. Posture is autobiography, an external embodiment of our inner state. It records and explains what we did and who we are.

Your distinctive postural profile exposes all secrets of commission, omission, and submission. Don't worry—the evidence is not admissible in a court of law. Yet it is extraordinarily useful if you want to be truly free of pain, depression, self-doubt, and self-destructive habits.

We already looked at the fact collector personality type; the second personality type is the skeptic, who is fated to live a life in doubt.

The skeptic expects to be cheated. The world, he is sure, is full of bandits, incompetents, and hidden pitfalls. Only the vigilant, the canny, the tough survive. He armor-plates his ego and refuses to be lured out into the open, where his superior IQ might be defeated by trickery or bad luck.

Skeptics are indeed smart. Quick witted and usually well educated, they can be fun to be around. But there is more darkness than light to their personality. Their cynical expectations rob them of their primary power and their greatest gifts: positive energy, joy, and peace of mind. When they come to the clinic, the typical skeptic is in pain. There is a postural condition (most likely) that has left them unbalanced and energy depleted. Without being directly conscious of it, they are afraid—afraid of illness, injury, aging, limitation. Their actions are intended to make fear easier to bear, but it actually makes things worse. Much worse.

The skeptic's mantra is a form of absolution, full of self-forgiveness and self-soothing: *I am not to blame; I was cheated by the system; I had no choice; I inherited my grandfather's high blood pressure.* There are many variations. Still, the skeptic can't escape the fear: *Since I am clearly not to blame, maybe I won't be punished.* Our egos punish us when we fall short of perfection. A perfect person does not get sick or injured. Of course that's nonsense, but our inner scold, a critic and all-around harpy, bedevils us with a steady stream of backseat driving.

She rationalizes her doubting, blame-shifting attitude as awareness and acceptance of personal responsibility. It seems safer and easier to hide behind a tough, know-it-all negativity than to face up to the responsibilities that come from putting herself out there. To the skeptic, it seems much harder to take on the tasks of recovering lost balance, retrieving lost knowing, and rediscovering peace of mind than sitting firmly behind the tough exterior.

As a postural therapist, skeptics used to give me fits. They have always been among the brightest of my clients, yet when they had completed an item from their menu of balancing E-cises and I asked how they felt, often the answer was, "Feels the same." I could see with one quick glance that the E-cises had done their work—the shoulder, hip, or whatever it was that had been misaligned was at least beginning to move back into its proper place. It surprised and baffled me that these patients didn't feel the effects. For many years, I assumed they were either willfully, perversely refusing to cooperate, or that some physiological mechanism was overriding what they should have been feeling.

By being patient and forcing myself to listen and observe closely, I detected that skeptics did feel the change; they simply did not trust it enough to acknowledge it to me or to themselves. What they felt came and went too fast, or didn't stand out against the background noise and distractions of their self-abnegation. The positive feelings associated with realignment seemed like the memories of a fleeting dream. I had to find a way to make those quick flashes of feeling good cohere into an enduring awareness.

A client, L.J., gave me the first breakthrough. There was pain in his right hip. I asked him to stand on his right foot with the left leg bent at the knee. In this position, the left foot could be stretched back to allow the toes to hook behind him on the front edge of a waist-high countertop.* He had been standing that way for three minutes. When I asked him to put both feet back on the floor and move his right hip a little to see if it still hurt, he muttered flippantly, "Dream on." As soon as his foot was off the countertop, though, his eyes widened in disbelief.

"Well?" I asked.

"Same."

It was a complete lie. Actually, it was an incomplete lie—L.J.'s eyes revealed the truth. The E-cise had repositioned his hip, putting his pelvis in a level (right to left) position instead of dropping away to the right, which left the hip joint grinding in the socket. Rather than challenge him, I surrendered, or at least I pretended to. "I guess you've stumped me." I went on to say something to the effect that what the clinic was offering just wasn't right for him and that we would refund his money. L.J. immediately rejected the offer and suggested that I was being too hasty and that maybe, now that he had a chance to think about it, he could feel a change in his hip.

That was the buy-in I was looking for. Instead of closing the sale, I borrowed a little of his cynicism: "Just got lucky, I guess." That response endures to this day whenever we deal with a skeptic in one of our clinics. I advise my therapists not to attack the story—instead, I

---

* If you try this E-cise and have trouble getting the back leg into position, use the seat of a chair instead of a countertop. Stand straight with your head and shoulders back. Keep the hips even and level. Use the back of another chair to help keep your balance. If you are having problems with this one, it confirms that you need a lot of work on your hips.

recommend that they ride it home in triumph. *Just got lucky* is okay with me. After thinking it over, very soon the skeptic—make that the former skeptic—will realize it too.

I have always suspected that even self-proclaimed cynics (what I like to call "skeptics on steroids") never completely succeed in fooling themselves into believing their own cynicism. They are actually seeking confirmation in the form of road-tested personal experience that it is safe to have faith. We all know that having faith in oneself is the source of peace of mind. Knowing that we are enough is indeed enough. Thoughts, even cynical ones, pertain to a human being's role in co-creating his or her own health. By not immediately requiring a cynic to buy into the need for an unshakable faith in self, I am briefly sharing their story, their secret, and allowing them to be present and aware of what's taking place. It won't be long before this causes the cynical story to fall away, revealing the truth.

Skeptics look as if they are moving sideways—and they are. They use their wits and deep distrust to slip around obstacles. A shoulder or a hip, often both, are rotated forward and to the left, which gives skeptics, both male and female, an appearance of drifting off at an angle as they walk forward. And they *would* drift without some artful counter-torquing by their knees, by the sockets of the hip joints, and by head fake-outs (tilting, turning, and thrusting) that serve as rudders to keep them on course.

Am I saying that there is a skeptic musculoskeletal system type that is paired with the corresponding personality type? Yes.

Take a Plane

If the musculoskeletal system is fully functional, your major load-bearing joints are in horizontal and vertical planar alignment. A plane is a boundless flat surface of infinite extent and no thickness, encompassing three or more points not on a straight line.

Our posture reveals how we move. How we move is who we are. Skeptics' movement is based on trying to protect their heart, both as a working pump and the place where love, courage, and generosity dwell. A skeptic feels extremely vulnerable advancing straight at the world with his precious heart, spiritual and otherwise, exposed; consequently, he adopts a defensive posture by rotating the pelvis and the upper torso so that the shoulders and rib cage shield the heart. This rotation is the crux of musculoskeletal system dysfunction. It disrupts the vertical load-bearing alignment that allows us to move forward smoothly in a straight line, change direction without losing our balance, hop on one foot, carry a load, and, in general, get around without mishap and injury. The precisely calibrated, invisible scaffolding that makes us one of the most mobile creatures on earth is comprised of the alignment of and interaction between just a few planes. The four horizontal parallel planes of the body consist of those created by the shoulders, the hips, the knees, and the ankles/feet. When combined with two vertical parallel planes formed by the paired load joints (right or left shoulder, hip, knee, and ankle/foot), the mobile body is formed.

By rotating her shoulders and hips, a skeptic disrupts her balance. To avoid falling, she resorts to a variety of dodges that strain her muscles, damage her joints, and severely limit her range of movement. At the same time, this creates a distinct, misaligned, non-vertical posture that is mistakenly regarded as a family trait, lifestyle choice, random selection, or aging.

When you lose your vertical and horizontal integrity, the posture displayed is a symptom of illness. It may not hurt yet, but it soon will. The dysfunctional posture is interfering with the body's need for healthy, unrestricted movement, and it is relentlessly undermining vital physiological processes.

Natural, unrestricted movement allows several degrees of smooth, spontaneous, rotating motion both horizontally and vertically. It serves as a regulating mechanism that will continue as long as the bones involved can return to rest in neutral. There's nothing wrong with rotation; in an emergency we may need extra flexibility to avoid stumbling or to jump out of harm's way. Incomplete rotation is the problem—frozen, stuck, jammed rotation that never returns to neutral and thereby prevents muscles from resetting for repeated contractions.

Skeptics are always rotated; usually right to left so that the heart is pulled back with the right shoulder and side interposed toward the front. As I pointed out in *The Egoscue Method of Health Through Motion*, you can see the rotation in the mirror. One shoulder or hip looks closer than the other. If there is shoulder or hip rotation (or both, which is common), your posture is off balance.

Repeat after me: *the body is a unit*. It is an important mantra.

Everything is connected to everything else. If your shoulders are rotated, that affects your spine. Your spine affects your head, and your head's position affects vision, balance, hearing, and neural functions. And that's just for openers—rotated shoulders have an impact on the lower back and the hips too. The hips are in close collaboration with the knees, the ankles, and feet.

I used to rely on the pain-on/pain-off approach. I thought that turning off the pain by eliminating the rotation would convince a client that the restoration of postural balance was the cure he or she sought. I didn't understand that the skeptic's need to protect the heart took precedence. Their fear of being deceived, tripped up, and trapped blocked their awareness. They stuck with their story unless I gave them time and encouragement to realize that by being fully balanced there was no danger that they couldn't surmount.

I set out to create a non-threatening atmosphere that allows balance to slowly re-emerge for the skeptic. Without undergoing the humiliation and fear, they gradually wean themselves away from the need for their story. By becoming balanced, plugging back into the universal power grid, re-energizing, and being present in the moment, they gain peace of mind. They've got energy, strength, calmness, gratitude, and great joy. How do they know? They feel it.

★　★　★　★　★

Are you a skeptic? Do any of the following apply to you?

- You've been saying "Bull!" throughout this chapter.
- You're no cynic, just a "contrarian."
- You've already sampled some of the E-cises and don't think they seem very effective.
- You bought one of my other books and your back, knee, shoulder, or whatever still hurts . . . so this book must be more of the same old, same old.
- You regard life as ugly, brutish, and short.
- You are a pessimist, or maybe an optimist? Or is it a little of both? Maybe you don't even know.
- Your body is letting you down. Or are you letting your body down? (Was that a stupid question?)
- You wonder if it is too late for you.
- You're not sure what kind of personality you have or what you believe in.
- You're not sure what hurts or why.
- You haven't looked at yourself in the mirror lately, especially not in a full-length mirror. If you did, perhaps you didn't like what you saw or didn't know what to do about what you saw.
- You don't know how you feel or why.

Take a long, leisurely walk. Think about those questions and answer two or three of them. By the time you get back home, decide if you are a skeptic. If you are, do the E-cises that follow. If you decide that you are not a skeptic—and that is entirely possible—go on to the next chapter.

To learn more about the exercises in this chapter, please refer to the E-Cise Menu for Skeptics on the Pain Free Living *DVD.*

E-cise Menu for Skeptics

FOOT CIRCLES/POINT FLEXES

This E-cise restores ankle flexibility and strengthens the flexion and extension muscles. For Foot Circles, lie on your back with one leg extended flat on the floor and the other bent with the knee toward the chest. Clasp your hands behind the bent knee while you circle the foot clockwise 20 times. Meanwhile, keep the other leg on the floor with toes pointing straight toward the ceiling. Reverse the direction of the circling foot and repeat. Change sides and repeat, making sure the knee stays absolutely still, with the movement coming from the ankle, not the knee.

For Point Flexes, stay in the same position on your back with one leg extended and the other bent. Bring the toes of the extended leg toward the shin to flex the foot, then reverse the direction to point the foot. Do 20 flex/point combos, then repeat with the other foot for another 20 (40 total) reps.

SITTING FEMUR ROTATIONS

This E-cise introduces full lateral movement of the knee and ankle via the hip socket. Sit on the floor with both legs extended straight in front of you. Your feet should be 8 to 10 inches apart. For support, place your hands behind your hips by about 4 inches. Tighten your thigh muscles, flex your toes, and roll your hips forward to arch your back. Using your hip sockets, rotate your knees and feet inward and then outward. It is important to keep your hips rolled forward, with thighs and toes flexed. Do not lean back too heavily on your hands; try to sit up straight with your head and shoulders back. Each rotation-in-and-rotation-out combo counts as a repetition. Do 3 sets of 20 reps.

CROCODILE TWIST

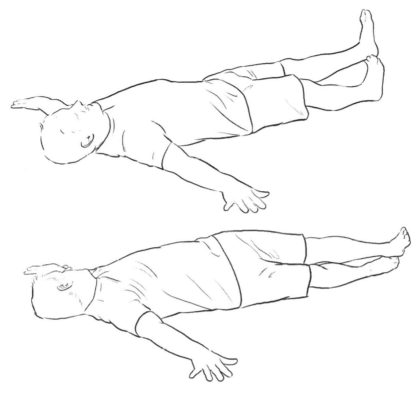

This E-cise promotes bilateral activity by wringing out the posture muscles of the spine and the hip, making them contract and release equally on both sides. Lie on your back with legs extended flat on the floor. Point the toes of your right foot at the ceiling, heel on the floor. Put the heel of your left foot on the toes of your right foot (the right big toe will be the primary contact point). Extend your arms to the side, level with the shoulders, palms facing the floor. Tighten the thigh muscles (quadriceps) of both legs and roll your feet to the right, getting them to touch the floor, while keeping one foot aligned atop the other. As you do this, lift your left hip off the floor, pointing it at the ceiling. Your head looks to the left (get your ear as close to the floor as possible). Hold this position for 1 minute and breathe; keep the thighs tight. Reverse the feet and repeat on the other side for 1 minute.

CATS AND DOGS

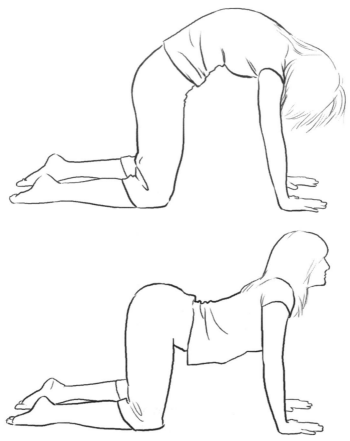

This E-cise works the hips, spine, shoulders, and neck in coordinated flexion-extension. Get down on the floor on your hands and knees, making sure that your knees are aligned with your hips, wrists, and shoulders, and that your lower legs are parallel with each other and with your hips. Evenly distribute your weight. Smoothly round your back as your head curls down to create a curve that runs from the buttocks to the neck—this is the cat with an arched back. Smoothly sway the back down while bringing the head up—this is the perky dog. Make these two moves flow continuously back and forth rather than allowing them to be distinct and choppy. Do 10 repetitions, with each cat-and-dog combo counting as a single rep.

STANDING AT WALL WITH PILLOW BETWEEN KNEES

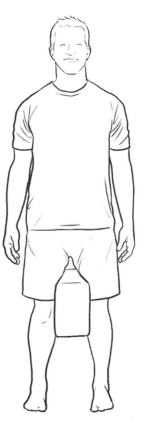

This E-cise promotes proper positioning of all load joints. Stand at a wall with your feet parallel and hips-width apart. Your heels, hips, upper back, and *maybe* your head are against a wall. (*Maybe,* because some people have severe shoulder rotation and/or slumping, which pull the neck and head forward. If so, bring your head up and back toward the wall as far as it will go without forcing it. Over time as you do this E-cise, the muscles will gradually strengthen enough to bring the back of your head into contact with the wall.) Relax your stomach muscles and make sure that your feet remain pointed straight ahead. A small, inflatable pillow or block between your knees should feel as if it is slightly pushing the knees apart. Do not push into the pillow; it is there to trigger some of your hip muscles to provide stabilization while you are in this position. Hold for 4 minutes.

STATIC EXTENSION POSITION

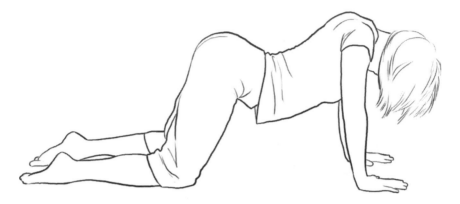

This E-cise counteracts hip rotation. Start on your hands and knees on the floor. Move your hands forward by about 6 inches, then move your upper body forward so that your shoulders are above your hands. Your hips are now in front of your knees by about 6 inches. Keep your elbows straight, and allow your shoulder blades to collapse together while your low back arches as your hips roll forward. Drop your head and stay in this position for 3 minutes.

SITTING KNEE PILLOW SQUEEZES

This E-cise promotes bilateral pelvic extension and encourages pelvic stability. Sit toward the front edge of a hard chair (don't lean into the chair back) with a thick pillow or inflatable block between your knees, and your pelvis rolled forward to put an arch in your lower back. Keep your feet pointed straight ahead and your upper body relaxed. Squeeze and release the pillow between your knees; keep the arch in your low back. Remember, your feet are pointed straight ahead. Do 3 sets of 20 repetitions.

SITTING ABDUCTOR PRESS WITH STRAP

This E-cise develops bilateral pelvic extension and encourages pelvic stability. A four-foot-long, non-elastic strap with a buckle is needed for this E-cise (or you can improvise with an old belt or a length of rope). Sit in a chair with your feet pointed straight ahead. Buckle or tie the strap around your knees, with your knees hips-width apart, and your pelvis rolled forward to put an arch in your lower back. Do not lean back. Maintaining the spinal arch, push outward against the strap at your knees and release. Do 3 sets of 20 repetitions.

STANDING ARM CIRCLES

This E-cise strengthens the muscles of the upper back that are involved with the shoulders' ball-and-socket function. Stand facing a full-length mirror with your feet parallel and toes pointing straight ahead. Place a pillow or inflatable block between your knees. Curl your fingertips into the pads of each palm (the fleshy area at the base of the fingers), and point your thumbs straight out. (This hand position, called the "golfer's grip," is imperative to the success of this E-cise.) Squeeze your shoulder blades together, and bring your arms out to the sides at shoulder level, elbows straight. With your palms facing down and thumbs pointed forward, circle up and forward. With your arms still out at shoulder level and palms up, circle up and back. Remember to keep your wrists, arms, and elbows straight, with the shoulder blades squeezed together. Don't contract your stomach muscles—the circles must come from the shoulders. Keep your neck and head back. Do 100 forward repetitions and 100 back repetitions.

TWELVE

MAKING THE WORST OF IT

PESSIMISTS DON'T JUST TELL THEIR STORY—they are their story. Pessimists are certain that they live under an unrelenting siege. They collect the damned and the unlucky things that have happened in their lives and bolt them together to serve as both a script and as an alibi for their lives. Pessimists think and talk about:

- How bad things happen to a good person.
- Why the worst case trumps the best of intentions.
- The addicting thrill of identifying the one who bears the blame for all the pain, limitation, and despair.

Yes, a pessimist's story is a litany of woe that goes from one negative incident to another, event by event, typically covering ten to twenty years of soap opera–like plot development in which boundless hope, the most powerful medicine of all, gives way to oppressive negativity. But that's no soap opera—it's the stuff of real, personal tragedy and searing emotional pain.

No, I should have known better.

No, that was a mistake.

No . . . I'm afraid it's too late.

Pessimists are willing to take long treks into the distant past to relive accidents, illnesses, disappointments, and assorted mishaps.

They pass harsh judgment on themselves and others, wallow in recriminations, and fulminate at the injustice. Their stories are epic and comprehensive. Great heaps of rubble block the way and keep the narrator-protagonist from either moving forward to a fresh start or toward taking responsibility for their own history and health.

Pessimists can recover their positive energy flow, peace of mind, and perfect health only by putting down the burden of their woeful story and reopening a connection to the present. It's not easy. But you can do it. You are enough.

★   ★   ★   ★   ★

When I was a young Marine second lieutenant in Vietnam, my commanding officer got fed up with my indecision during a firefight. It was my first time leading troops in combat, and as I conferred with him on the field radio, I dithered back and forth between options. He barked at me, "Make up your mind, lieutenant . . . don't die wondering." That was good advice. So stop wondering. If you're unsure, assume you are a pessimist, so you can do something about it.

In the clinic, we help pessimists put down their burdensome stories by reintroducing postural balance, which always calms the mind and restores the flow of positive energy. If I were forced to do triage, I would turn away the fact collectors and the skeptics and work only with the pessimists. They are in the deepest trouble.

Usually someone living in a bubble of pessimism becomes offended by the suggestion that he is to blame, even though no such implication was intended. The story, while deeply disturbing, is familiar and comforting. It's a security blanket and, rather than give it up, the skeptic backs off, loses interest in the Egoscue Method, makes excuses, or starts arguing. Perversely, he is proud of his story and fiercely protective of it. After all, he is at the center of the tale, heroically enduring outrageous slings and arrows.

Parsing Pronouns

A word or two about gender and pronouns: I switch genders to establish that personality types are common in both men and women. No gender has a monopoly on any characteristic or personality. Pronouns are totally interchangeable.

Pessimists love show-and-tell—the more dramatic, the better. Their story is on a conversational loop that plays and replays. Even so, I'm willing to listen to a story over and over again, waiting for the opportunity to ask, "What would you like to do now?"

Often, the answer is something like, "I just don't know. I've tried everything."

"You told me that your neck hurts—nine and a half on a ten-point scale. Since you are here today, do you think it makes sense to see if we can knock that down a little—say to a six or seven—if we can?"

"I don't know. You can try. . . ."

Cue the fireworks, the balloon drop, and confetti. In the initial phase of working with the pessimist, "I don't know. You can try. . . ." is as good as it gets. He doesn't have the energy to invest in even low-grade enthusiasm. He is running on empty. The remarkable thing is that he is even running at all. Their stories have blotted out every survival instinct except one last trace of hope. Instead of quitting, they hang on to a last vestige of against-the-odds belief—belief, not in themselves, but in the experts whom they have turned to for aid. This is a mixed blessing, but if that's what we've got to work with—so be it.

High Hopes

When a pessimist first arrives at one of our clinics, she is certain we will rescue her from pain. Tommy was a good example. He had researched the Egoscue Method and was convinced it was the silver bullet. Yet that certainty was undermined by his conviction that he would screw it up. Why? His story proved it. Time and time again, he had consulted the best minds of medicine and health care, mainstream, experimental, and alternative practitioners who have stellar reputations and solid track records. He followed their advice, underwent unpleasant treatments, and dutifully submitted to expensive tests, intrusive examinations, and patronizing lectures. It was typical. Undaunted on the surface, our pessimist friend kept at it, but the only things to show for his effort were more pain, less energy, and another chapter to add to his story about a man who tried and failed. There is no way to argue the pessimist out of this poisonous mind-set. He listened intently, nodded gravely, and said, "What you're saying has merit, but I just don't know."

And how right he was! He didn't know. He had to feel his way to positive expectations that can serve as the fulcrum for action. By gently nudging the pessimist toward deciding to take action based on what he feels, and by framing it in low-key terms, I leave the story in place without directly disputing the failure expectation that is its foundation. Openly challenging his self-defeating story would provoke a stubborn defense that usually leaves the pessimist opting to go elsewhere for help rather than give up his story. If I want him to stick with me and decide to take the next step, it has to be his choice. Typically, experts like to make decisions. This is true of experts of all sorts. Experts are professionally and emotionally invested in a treatment methodology, stand ready and eager to implement it, and assume—not at all unreasonably—that they are being consulted precisely to make those decisions.

Unawareness

Meditation and other similar techniques provide a means of conscious access to and awareness of actuating beliefs. Emotional turmoil is a consequence of one's inability to achieve an enlightened awareness.

In reality, pessimists want experts to validate their story *and* cure the problem, but that's impossible. Why? Human health is influenced by what I call *actuating belief*. Those who want help with their health have to accept that I'm in charge of their health. Total buy-in is required. To do that, however, the expert must repeal Existential Health Law number one:

Healing and health come from within the individual.

Passive bystanders and experts are outsiders by definition. Hence, a pessimist only *thinks* she believes that the expert is the answer to her prayers. What she actually believes is just the opposite. Her aware mind, not the thinking mind, instinctively embraces all the fundamental realities of existence because they actuate existence itself, thereby becoming forms of unalterable transcendent belief. An individual may not be enlightened enough to be consciously aware of an actuating belief, but his or her physiological systems are fully attuned. That's not to say that actuating beliefs shield us from the folly of our thinking minds or our inability to fully access the aware mind. The unaware—the unenlightened—pay a high price. They persist in taking actions (thoughts are both forms of action and forms of matter/energy) that undermine their health and well-being by diverting and draining off positive, high-wavelength energy.

By deferring to experts and handing over to them personal responsibility for her health, the pessimist loses important benefits that would otherwise reach her by way of the actuating and actionable belief that health comes from within. She is closing down a vital feedback loop that provides energy, strength, and confidence. If this happened only occasionally or temporarily, it wouldn't be a big deal. The human body has a genius for problem solving and coping with the unexpected, but when experts take charge by orchestrating onslaughts of toxic chemical compounds and traumatic surgical intervention, on top of a modern culture that features poor nutritional standards and acutely sedentary lifestyles, the cumulative damage can be enormous and lasting.

It is not possible to simultaneously believe and disbelieve, which is what the pessimist attempts to do. As powerful as the thinking mind is, it cannot erase existential belief derived from biological reality. Thoughts are things. The thought, confirmed by the experience of allowing the expert to usurp power, delivers the message *you are not enough*, and that attitude suppresses healing when a pessimist is chased away from her rightful, paramount role as the primary health generator and guardian. That's what I mean when I use the term "actuating belief." By believing in the expert and disbelieving her own power, she ends up losing the very thing she depends on to guarantee health and well-being.

Belief is the mind's thumb. Like the thumbs of our hands, which allow us the flexibility, control, strength, and delicate touch to make and grasp tools, belief gives us the power to use the mind in a deliberate and structured way. It links thought to action. If you do not believe there are fish in the pond, you won't go fishing. Indeed, the practical effect is the same no matter what the actual conditions—no fish. If you don't believe that the aspirin will get rid of your headache, you probably won't take it. If you believe the chemotherapy will kill you before it cures your cancer, you probably will refuse it.

Belief can serve as an on-off switch that activates or deactivates important supporting physiological mechanisms. Notice that I use the word "supporting." Medical treatment isn't magic; mostly it is chemistry or, in the case of surgery, sophisticated forms of carpentry and plumbing. Hit living tissue with a hammer and it reacts, but after that happens, then what? Physical discomfort, pain, and health in general are extremely subjective states. Our senses receive stimuli that lack a uniform objective basis because sensory perception is unique to the individual. Humans raise physical sensation to the level of perception by assigning meaning and value to a biochemical and neurological event that involves impingement on receptor cells of a sensory organ such as the eye, ear, or skin. A vast range of sensory mechanisms is only now beginning to be fully appreciated by cutting-edge science.

By transferring responsibility to the expert, a pessimist sits back and waits to feel a positive or negative sensation. And waits and waits and waits. Deep down, he really expects the negative. What he thinks he believes in, usually half-heartedly—the expert's educational credentials and state-of-the-art tools—are unlikely to produce a sensation capable of overcoming the pervasive fear that is blocking the flow of positive energy he needs to regain health. The body's internal scanning mechanism finds only an overactive thinking mind coping with an idea—powerlessness—that is at odds with biological experience.

Am I saying that all medical and expert-managed intervention is ineffective? No. But effectiveness is a direct consequence of the individual's belief system. In the case of the pessimist, that belief system is impaired by an expectation of failure, much of it generated by a story that neatly "confirms" that an ineffective outcome is inevitable. Successes that occur are a result of treatment that just happens to get under the radar of those negative expectations, principally by triggering deep-seated unconscious beliefs (and their supporting positive emotions) that manage to operate independently of the failure expectations and counteract their deadly effects.

Access to the aware mind is of great importance. By putting the pessimist back in charge of her expectations and her health through reestablishing postural balance, it is possible to place her at the center of things, where she can decide to take up her responsibilities instead of handing them off to outsiders. Restoration of postural balance won't happen all at once and may not happen at all. Even so, it is essential to try to move in the right direction, to encourage the pessimist to resume taking small portions of responsibility, which can be gradually expanded. It is a way to slowly regain lost confidence, ratchet down the sense of helplessness, muzzle the fear of powerlessness, and begin to rebuild the capacity to absorb positive energy.

You can feel it! You'll know when it's time to drop that story.

Pessimists have lost their aware minds. The obsession with story blocks awareness by leading them back into the past and/or ahead into the future (usually both). Only the present is energized, however. Every moment that the mind spends outside of the present by rehashing events and situations that no longer exist as a way to learn from mistakes—which is really an excuse to find fault with oneself—is a moment disconnected from the universal energy grid. Similarly, imagining future events that will most likely never take place also cuts her off from the supply of high-wavelength energy that would restore her balance. Pessimists are in the habit of reliving the past and pre-living the future. Consequently, they are in an acute state of energy deprivation.

Their despair is palpable. In *The Egoscue Method of Health Through Motion*, I described Condition IIIs as having the posture of despair: hips tilted under as though a pair of hands had gripped them from behind and yanked them forward and then down with tremendous force. This flattens the S-curve of the spine. The "S" is actually reversed (like this: 2) so that when the pelvis tilts under, the lower curve no longer bellies to the left. This left curve is what gives us spinal strength, balance, and flexibility. This sends the shoulders forward, rounded and slumped, and leaves the head to jut forward. It is the signature posture of the pessimist. Stiff and unbalanced, she struggles to stay upright as gravity seeks to topple her to the earth face-first. Her shoulders and knees torque and wobble to keep her moving forward in a straight line. She trips and falls frequently. Walking is stressful, climbing stairs is agonizing, and running rips up joints and courts a heart attack. A pessimist's lifestyle is not to blame, heredity has little to do with it, and there's nothing wrong with the design of her body. This looks like energy starvation—and it *is* energy starvation. The pessimist is very familiar. She looks like your neighbor, daughter, boss. Glance in the mirror; she may look like you.

When asked how they feel right now, pessimists don't have the vocabulary handy to describe the present moment, so they launch into a report on what their physician believes is wrong, the latest side effects of the medicine and the headaches that interfere with their resolutions to get more exercise and a good night's sleep. These stories are layered with symptoms, tests, mistakes, and unforeseen complications.

I'll respond: "No, that's how you felt last week when you went to see the doctor. How do you feel right now?"

"The same."

"Tell me how the 'same' feels."

"It hurts."

"Where?"

Pessimists seem almost reluctant to pinpoint the pain. The reason is that a specific locus of pain has morphed and diffused into a general sensation that is part pain, part fear, part metabolic slowdown, and part physiological exhaustion. Pessimists are flooded with incoming calls from their internal sensors, warning that their system is sliding into a catastrophic state of deterioration. Actual pain—the I-can't-bend-my-knee without-screaming kind of pain— is the least of their worries.

Most pessimists have gotten accustomed to feeling lousy, but it is impossible to fake a sunny outlook on life. They are glum, anxious, and weary. When I ask where it hurts, the idea of being able to focus on a single ache or pain seems strange. It would make more sense to ask where it *doesn't* hurt. They have come to expect to feel bad, and deal with it by treating their symptoms like cantankerous old friends or beloved pets that must be coddled and indulged; otherwise they'll act up and behave badly. As for the future, they don't anticipate a change for the better.

There is a reverse placebo effect (known as the nocebo effect) that pessimists bring into the offices of health-care practitioners of every stripe that makes progress extremely unlikely. If a patient believes the visit will help make him feel better, he will actually show signs of improvement a day or so before the visit takes place: a classic placebo effect. But when the pessimist believes that nothing will help—guess what? Nothing helps. The powers of intention, attention, and expectation have enormous effect. Thoughts are things. The body responds to the mind by adjusting blood and brain chemistry, altering the permeability of cellular membranes and increasing oxygen flow. A third power, the power of awareness, is at work too. By tuning out the present and focusing instead on her story filled with shadows of the past, a pessimist cannot marshal her full physical and mental resources. In Shakespeare's *Henry IV, Part 1*, the mouthy Welsh warlord Glendower brags that he can win a crucial battle by calling on supernatural powers from the "vasty deep."

"Why, so can I, or so can any man," replies Hotspur, who then asks blandly, "but will they come when you do call?" A pessimist's formidable inner powers may never hear the call to join in today's battle because she is looking toward the past, not the present. As a result, the forces of hope and life do not come to the rescue. Worse, they are actively turned away.

Energy surrounds and saturates all living things like the sea that washes around a coral reef, bathing, nurturing, and healing its teeming efflorescence. The living reef is embraced by the sea's life-giving energy; it opens itself to the current and lives. The embrace is all. As long as the powers of intention, attention, expectation, and awareness are switched off or pointed elsewhere, there can be no transfer of energy, no embrace, and soon—no life.

The thrilling thing about pessimists is that they can turn on a dime once they get a little traction. By putting their story aside for as little as ten minutes while they concentrate on a few basic balancing exercises, a rush of incoming energy can blast the pessimist out of the hole she has dug for herself. The present floods in and saturates her with a sense of well-being.

By encouraging pessimists to take small, simple steps to restore musculoskeletal system balance without tying it to the story one way or the other (if the story is never heard of again, good riddance!), a postural therapist can quickly help boost their metabolism and send their mood soaring. In short order, the pessimist's story starts losing relevance and power. Within a very few days, as her postural balance improves, she finds that her focus has shifted away from her story and onto the present. Her aware mind blossoms; fear no longer stalks her. She marvels at the enjoyment derived from a short walk to visit friends and a brisk stroll on the beach at low tide to collect shells, something she hasn't done for years. You are enough after all.

Come on, give it a try. Embrace the present moment. Always catch the rain.

To learn more about the exercises in this chapter, please refer to the E-Cise Menu for Pessimists on the Pain Free Living *DVD.*

E-cise Menu for Pessimists

STANDING PIGEON-TOED AT THE WALL

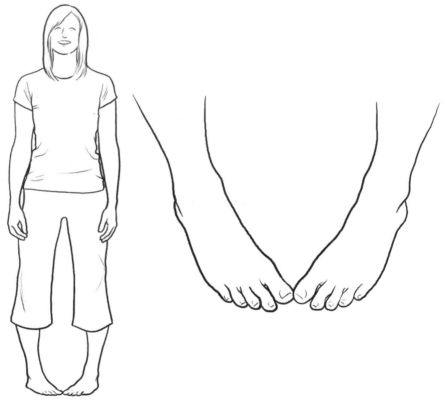

This E-cise is for proper pelvic tilt. Stand with your heels, buttocks, back, shoulders, and your head against the wall. Feel both your shoulder blades against the wall. Make sure the back of your head contacts the wall and that you are not arching your shoulders. Feet should be parallel and about hips-width apart. Swivel your feet inward so that the big toes touch, and maintain this angle during the E-cise. Relax your stomach and take deep breaths. If your head won't stay against the wall, roll up a towel or use an inflatable roll and put it between your neck and the wall. Keep your hands at your sides, thumbs facing forward. Hold for 4 to 6 minutes.

IN-LINE GLUTEAL CONTRACTIONS

This E-cise works the glute muscles (*musculus gluteus*) in the buttocks for proper movement of the feet, to keep the pelvis from tipping forward, and to allow leg extension for stair climbing. Stand with the heel of your left foot touching the tips of your right toes. The feet will be flat on the floor and in a straight line, with knees locked. Balance your hips evenly to the right and left (they may want to rotate and swing your torso around) by equalizing your weight on both feet and keeping your head and shoulders back. Simultaneously contract and release both the right and left glutes. Do 3 sets of 20. Switch the feet (right in front of left), contract, and release the glutes for another 3 sets of 20. Don't use your abdominal muscles. Make the contractions full, smooth, and slow. If you have trouble retaining your balance, use a chair or a wall for support.

STANDING FORWARD BEND

This E-cise loosens the hamstring muscles. Place your feet flat on the floor, parallel and about hips-width apart. Slowly bend over at the waist, knees straight, touching your fingertips to the floor (or as far as you can get), head hanging. Breathe. Feel the stretch equally in the back of both legs but don't force it. Hold for 1 minute.

To come out of the exercise, unlock your knees, letting them move toward the floor as the hips release and the upper torso dips forward and upward. Or, as you unlock your knees, rest your hands on the thighs just above the knees, unlock the knees, and transfer the weight from your lower back to your hands. Push upward, arch your back, and shift your weight back toward the hips. With level hips, lift the upper torso into an upright, fully vertical position.

STATIC EXTENSION POSITION

This E-cise counteracts hip rotation. Start on your hands and knees on the floor. Move your hands forward by about 6 inches, then move your upper body forward so that your shoulders are above your hands. Your hips are now in front of your knees by about 6 inches. Keep your elbows straight, and allow your shoulder blades to collapse together while your low back arches as your hips roll forward. Drop your head and stay in this position for 3 minutes.

CATS AND DOGS

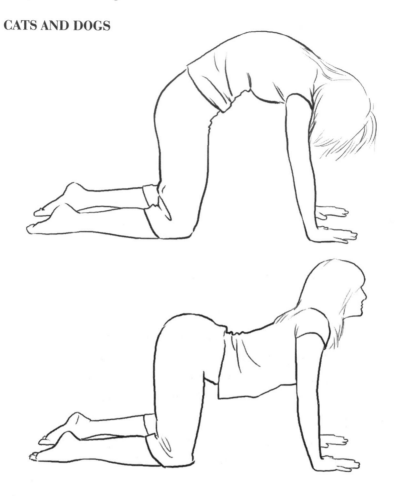

This E-cise works the hips, spine, shoulders, and neck in coordinated flexion-extension. Get down on the floor on your hands and knees, making sure that your knees are aligned with your hips, wrists, and shoulders, and that your lower legs are parallel with each other and with your hips. Make sure your weight is distributed evenly. Smoothly round your back as your head curls down to create a curve that runs from the buttocks to the neck—this is the cat with an arched back. Smoothly sway the back down while bringing the head up—this is the perky dog. Make these two moves flow continuously back and forth rather than allowing them to be distinct and choppy. Do 10 repetitions, with each cat-and-dog combo counting as a single rep.

DOWNWARD DOG

This E-cise re-establishes linkage from the wrists to the feet. Assume the perky dog position in the Cats and Dogs exercise (see the opposite page). Curl your toes under, and push with your legs to raise your torso until you are off your knees with the weight resting on your hands and feet. Keep pushing until your hips are higher than your shoulders and have formed a tight, stable triangle with the floor. Your knees should be straight, your calves and thighs tight. Keep your feet pointing straight ahead in line with your hands, and not creeping backward. Your back should be flat, not bowed, as your hips press up and back into the heels. Breathe. If you cannot bring your heels flat onto the floor, get them as close as possible. Don't force them. It may take several sessions before they go all the way down. Remain in this position for 1 minute.

TOWEL-ROLL SETTLE WITH STRAP

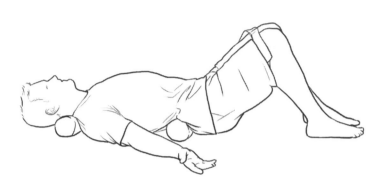

This E-cise allows gravity to relax and release the muscles of the upper body. You'll need two rolled bath towels. Lie on your back with knees bent and held together with a belt or nonelastic strap. Your feet should be flat on the floor and placed parallel about hips-width apart. Place one of the rolled towels under the back of your neck (don't rest your head on it; it is there to support your neck) and the other under your lower back just above the hips. Hold this position for 10 minutes.

CATS AND DOGS
See the instructions on page 130.

★   ★   ★   ★   ★

Don't rush through these; take your time and enjoy them.

THIRTEEN

UNSTICK THIS

OKAY. THE BIG THREE.

You're up—it's time to make a decision and take action.

Sonya, a well-known Hollywood actor, faced the same challenge after making only three visits to my San Diego clinic. She was hesitating and when I asked her what she wanted to do, she immediately replied, "Whatever you say."

I guess we know where she was coming from—straight from Planet Pessimism. What I said to her also applies to you, no matter where you are coming from: "Why not go with whatever the body says?"

Fortunately, he or she who hesitates is not lost, just bogged down. Start getting unstuck right here by answering a couple of easy questions: *How do you feel after doing each of the E-cise menus that I introduced in Chapters 10, 11, and 12? What happened physically and emotionally when you read them over and—most important—when you tried them?* Focus. You've just finished stimulating what amounts to the most sensitive, hyper-responsive life form that has ever existed. From the soles of your feet to the top of your skull there was (and still is) an uproar of signals, enzyme releases, hormone drips, adjustments, and status reports. More than 100 million protein molecules per cell are being concocted, dissolved, and re-assembled at any given instant. It is absurd to think that such an intricate, hair-trigger device just sits there dead in the water.

I believe the aware mind can dial in to any single cell in the body to receive a precisely detailed weather report. Yes, you can fine-tune your awareness to listen in on all this and infinitely more. Even if you are dealing with a serious chronic illness, the content of the message traffic is overwhelmingly positive. Only a tiny fraction of the content is reporting anomalies. Our earliest ancestors joyfully belly-flopped into the torrent of positive data and were carried for tens of thousands of years straight into adventures that drove other seemingly superior life-forms into extinction. Sadly, as of late, the trip has taken us on a detour from brash self-confidence to the doorstep of self-loathing. But we are in the process of getting back on the main highway.

★ ★ ★ ★ ★

And your decision is . . . ?

Oh, you haven't done the E-cises yet. (If you have—good! Skip the next paragraph as your reward.)

I have been taking it easy, maybe too easy, on giving a lot of explicit instructions in each chapter, because I want you to call the shots. This isn't a cookbook that you can flip through, read a recipe, imagine how good it tastes, and then turn to the next recipe and the next. I use the term "menu" for a reason. For one thing, "routine" and "program" make it sound like drudgery. The allusion to eating is apt because you need to get the benefits of these E-cises into your system. If you don't actually sample the items on the menus, then you are letting your thinking mind control the play. This is where your story starts getting in the way. A fact collector is probably thinking, "I need more facts." The skeptic concludes, "It can't be that simple." And the pessimist hides out in his steadily shrinking comfort zones, muttering, "I can't do this myself." The plot always thickens. It is the reason our stories grow so large and cumbersome that eventually we are unable to move forward.

We all experience occasional brief bouts of indecision. However, chronic indecision is a symptom of a serious energy deficit. It takes a huge supply of energy to make important decisions and carry them out promptly, particularly those with many moving parts and potential complications. Individuals who are balanced, aware, and at peace with themselves effortlessly can draw on their abundant energy resources. Hence, decision making is no big deal. Any energy they use is promptly replaced. In contrast, when the fuel gauge is stuck on low, the tendency is to cut back on consumption; even small decisions seem enormous. When the energy shortage is prolonged—for those who are one of the three archetypal stories—the body is forced to retreat into the thinking mind. This substitutes various dodges such as *wait and see, pass the buck*, or general cynicism because other options requiring action further deplete the already inadequate amount of energy that remains available.

What we are trying to do is get you out of your thinking mind long enough to jump-start the flow of positive energy. You don't have to go into the E-cises cold; do a short series of warm-ups:

- Stand with your weight evenly distributed on each foot, eyes closed.
- Inhale and exhale deeply and slowly to a count of thirty.
- Listen to the sounds inside and outside the room.
- Imagine that you are looking down on yourself from above.
- Be grateful for the moment.

An important thing is taking place during these preliminaries: I am sneaking you extra energy, just enough to clear away the fog and engage your feeling mind. In addition, each item on the menu itself will supply a small spurt of energy as it restores (a little) postural alignment and balance.

One of these three menus will prompt your body to speak up louder and clearer than the others because the E-cises and their sequencing are having more impact on your musculoskeletal system's dysfunctions and misalignment. What's more, they are also getting through to your emotions and beginning to calm your mind. I suggest you try one—start with any of the three—and complete a different full menu each day for three days. On the third day, stand in a balanced position with your eyes closed, count slowly to thirty focusing on your breathing, and then, without pondering, choose. Just choose; don't try to explain, weigh, grade, or justify. Go with the menu that feels right.

What do I mean by "right"? That's a question I can't answer for you. You'll know it when you feel it.

Do that menu once a day for ten days. After each daily session, spend four or five minutes quietly listening to your body. Deliberately focus your attention on areas where there is pain, restriction, or limitation. It is not necessary to judge, evaluate, or compare; just become aware of the available sensations. Use this time to celebrate your body's many gifts.

The simple act of appreciation, of gratitude, can change the interior climate of the body from stressful to blissful. It is an antidote to the waves of fear that can roil the body and wreak havoc on the finely calibrated processes when we lose faith in our perfection. Pain is not an enemy. You have no enemies within unless you open the gates and invite them in.

Gate keeping is one of your body's most important functions. The membrane of each cell admits only carefully screened, beneficial material—that which has been signed, sealed, and delivered by evolution—while denying access to everything else. Cell biologist Bruce H. Lipton's brilliant research shows that the cell membrane scrutinizes the incoming matter in search of a key. When found, it activates the formation of a corresponding keyhole-and-lock mechanism (a necklace-like string of amino acids comprising a protein chain). The key opens a channel into the cell only if there is an exact match of key and keyhole. In other words, sustaining the cell with food, fuel, and other essentials is the work of the vigilant membrane—not DNA. The gate keeper closes the border when it detects danger. Hence, slight changes in valance, pH, turbidity, resonance, and a host of other subtle characteristics can lead to a protective cell lockdown.

Fear sends out powerful neurotransmitters that lead to the equivalent of a code-red alert. Apparently even imaginary fears, pessimism, doubts, habitual negativity, and anxiety can lead to partial or all-out restrictions in cellular access since such emotions may be legitimate symptoms of disease. The environment outside the cells, therefore, affects the environment within the cells. Blockading the resupply route into the cells, even if it is only a fraction of the entire sixty trillion, creates negative capability. Fundamentally, all actions are an expression of belief. Our beliefs—life is essentially good versus life is ugly, brutish, and short—essentially control our health by allowing expectation to express or distort perception. Bruce Lipton refers to it as "the Biology of Belief." He is exactly right.

Biologists use electron microscopes to discern cell behavior on this level; I contend that all you need is a mirror. In it is visible the tangible, physical expression of the biology of belief in the form of functional posture. If action is an expression of belief, posture is an expression of action(s). By way of original intent, posture's purpose is to effectuate common, everyday actions and fundamental belief—walking, running, throwing, stretching, embracing a mate, cuddling a child, striking an enemy, giving a gift to a friend, and so on—all expressions of fundamental belief in the wisdom of the body. One quick look at our posture tells us what we are capable or incapable of doing.

Glancing in the mirror—literally and figuratively, since we need no looking glass to truly know our posture—the perception processes of the body provide feedback on who we are and who we can be; our confidence ebbs and flows; and energy levels adjust. Best of all, posture is what-you-see-is-what-you-get. It provides an honest template of enormous potential and awesome nobility.

★　★　★　★　★

These E-cises have the power to switch postural awareness back on. You will feel the body responding to the stimulus and informing you about what is working and what isn't. Be patient. Expect success. If you are still uncertain, don't force it. Take a day or two off and then try again. As you run through the menu, note any changes. Is an E-cise harder than the last time? Easier?

Give the menu another full ten days. Meanwhile, bump up your physical activity levels. Go for a walk, work in the garden, dance. Monitor your moods, sleep, and appetite.

You should feel changes. If not, run through the same series of steps with the other menus.

···· FOURTEEN ····

WALL TO WALL, Y'ALL

═══════════════════════

I WOULD BE HUGELY DISAPPOINTED if this conversation of ours ended up lost in a thick fog of words. To avoid the danger of ending this process in confusion, I will invoke the "less is more" rule by turning to a classic technique for achieving brevity and clarity: the Chinese wall poster (my version).

First, an important adjuration (now there's a word from the thesaurus). Less is more when it comes to cool 1950s-ish Studebakers, Barcelona chairs, or Bauhaus-inspired office buildings. More is more when you are sucking up positive energy, balance, awareness, and motion. It is impossible to overindulge in the items on this menu. For every one of my wall posters add two or three or thirty of your own. Crank up the positive vibes. Go for it.

The human body teaches those
Who pay attention to put
Cynicism aside.

If something seems too good
To be true,
It probably is true.

*A symptom is part of a process,
Not an event.*

*Change
Is not something
To do.
You must allow
Change.*

Allow
Change
From the heart
And your head will
Follow.

Suffering
Is
Optional.

You are
Not
Broken.

*Ask
Why.*

Don't
Keep score,
Have fun.

Negative thoughts
Are the single worst
Health habit.

It is never as
Bad
As you think.

A path
Without obstacles
Has no destination.

You
Are pretty
Smart.
But your body is
Smarter.

A health expert
—Any health expert—
Cannot
Tell
You
Anything
You don't already know.

*Never fear
Yourself.*

*Pain is
The body's voice.
Listen
to
Your
Body.*

···· **FIFTEEN** ····

CONCLUSION

SOME AUTHORS END A BOOK WITH a carefully composed overview, or they offer up an inspiration to motivate the reader to apply the lessons they have learned.

But I'm going to rewind to Chapter 2 and push the "play" button.

★ ★ ★ ★ ★

Take off your shoes and socks. And stand up. Please.

Are you in the library or a bookstore? People are giving you funny looks as you remove your socks, aren't they? Don't worry—you won't get arrested.

★ ★ ★ ★ ★

Read the rest of this paragraph, and then shut your eyes and follow these instructions. Stand normally. Relax. Let your feet, shoulders, and head go where they want to go (and do go when someone isn't barking out orders). Keep your feet in place, and inhale and exhale a couple of times. Take your time. Notice how your weight is distributed. One leg may be working harder than the other. Is it the right leg? Or is it the left leg? Feel where the weight settles in the feet—is it in the heels? Maybe it's the inside edge, outside edge, or toward the toes. It's likely to be in a different spot for each foot. Let two or three minutes go by. Breathe.

Now, open your eyes. Read some more. Did you notice what was going through your mind when you were analyzing the weight distribution? Was there a jumble of ideas, images, and sensations?

A little of this and that? Quick, arrhythmic bursts of activity? A sensory jigsaw puzzle with a bunch of missing pieces? At the end of this paragraph, close your eyes again and pay attention to your mental traffic. Give it a minute and reopen your eyes.

Now, I'd like you to distribute your weight evenly. Read this paragraph and close your eyes again. Stand with both feet roughly parallel, pointing straight ahead and about hips-width apart. Now, turn them inward a little, until they are slightly pigeon toed. Easy does it. Carefully swing your torso, shoulders, and head around until you can feel the weight move in your feet.

Did you ever play flashlight tag as a kid? The beam of light moves like a disk, right? Your weight will have the same characteristic: it will focus and slide here and there. Nudge the disks into the balls of your feet. Bob a little at the knees, and tweak your hips. Some people will really have to crank themselves around. It may feel strange or precarious. Believe me, though, when the weight rests over the balls of the feet, your posture is in a balanced position. (The contortions and muscular effort to hold you there are necessary because your musculoskeletal structure is fighting to pop out of the temporary alignment I've put you in.) When you get the weight centered, notice how it feels, and notice what your mind is doing. Go ahead, try it.

When we have clients perform the same exercise in one of our Egoscue Method clinics, most of them say that in the first unbalanced position their minds are whirling, jumpy, and chaotic. They feel troubled, uncertain, uneasy. Balanced, however, is a different story. The mind calms down. It loses the jittery quality. There's more steadiness and clarity.

By changing your posture, you've changed your mind. The result is similar to switching channels on a radio or TV. A distant signal wavers and breaks up; adjusted to a closer, stronger frequency, the transmission sharpens and settles down.

INDEX

A

AAE patterns
   description of, 78
   fact collecting, 81, 82
   pessimism, 83
   skepticism, 82, 83
Action(s)
   and optimism 69, 70
   versus ideas, 51
Actuating belief, 118, 119
Adenosin diphosphate, 31
Adenosine triphosphate, 8, 9
Ankle flexibility, exercise for restoring,
   105
Attractor energy
   demonstration of, 67
   patterns, 52
Awareness
   as a generally recognized sense, 19
   of health, 38
   of pain, 16
   of time, 19

B

Back
   upper, exercise for releasing
      muscles, 132
   upper, exercises for strengthening
      muscles, 95, 113
Balance
   as a generally recognized sense, 19
   losing, 69
   musculoskeletal system and, 64
   postural, 65, 66
   what happens when it goes, 40
Balanced posture
   exercise, 22, 23
   and mind-body connection, 8
Balancing Act, 22, 23, 24–25, 26

Belief
   actuating, 118, 119
   and conditions within the body,
      46, 47
   and its role on pessimism, 120, 121
Big Bang Theory, 29, 30
The Biology of Belief, 19
Bryson, Bill, 24
The Bubble Universe, 30

C

Campbell, Joseph, ix, 5
Cats and dogs E-cise
   for fact collectors, 97
   for pessimists, 132
   for skeptics, 108
Cells
   "brain" of the, 8
   and posture change, 10
   power of, and longevity, 9
Chronic disease
   most reliable way of treating, 15
   and symptoms of pain, 16
Churchill, Winston, 45
Classical mechanics, 37
Columbus, and first recorded case of
   disorientation, iv
Conscious thought
   as a common human trait, 43
   as operational state of the mind,
      44
Crocodile twist E-cise, 107

D

Dalande, 30
Der Fliegende Holländer, 30
Desdemona, 3
Dinosaurs, extinction of, 34
Disorientation, iv
Downward dog E-cise, 128

E

E-cise menu
  cats and dogs, for fact collectors, 97
  cats and dogs, for pessimists, 130
  cats and dogs, for skeptics, 108
  crocodile twist, for skeptics, 107
  downward dog, for pessimists, 131
  foot circles, for skeptics, 105
  frog, for fact collectors, 94
  hip crossover, for fact collectors, 93
  hip lifts, for fact collectors, 92
  in-line gluteal contractions, for pessimists, 127
  knee-pollow squeezes in static back, 91
  point flexes, for skeptics, 105
  sitting abductor press with strap, for skeptics, 112
  sitting knee pillow squeezes, for skeptics, 111
  sitting femur rotations, for skeptics, 106
  standing arm circles, for fact collectors, 95
  standing arm circles, for skeptics, 113
  standing forward bend, for pessimists, 128
  standing pigeon-toed at the wall, for pessimists, 126
  standing quad stretch, 96
  standing at wall with pillow between knees, for skeptics, 109
  static back, for fact collectors, 90
  static extension position, for pessimists, 129
  static extension position, for skeptics, 110
  towel-roll settle with strap, for pessimists, 132
  warm-ups for, 135

Egoscue Method
  basis of, 4
  business trend in 1990s, 7
  design of, 57
  effectiveness of, 74
  for fact collectors, 90, 91–97
  and new clients, 45, 46
  as a non-medical postural therapy program, 5, 6
  and pain alleviation without surgery or drugs, 7
  for pessimists, 115–132
  and person with herniated disk, 12, 13
  purpose of, vi, vii, 57, 58
  for skeptics, 105–113
  worldwide reach of, vii
The Egoscue Method of Health Through Motion
  and three categories of musculoskeletal system dysfunction, 76, 77
  and posture of despair, 122
Einstein, Albert
  and most important life decision, 45
  and speed of light, 38
Emerson, Ralph Waldo, X
Emotional intelligence, 10
Emotions
  distilling from experience, 11, 12
  misuse of, v
  and turmoil, 118
Energy
  characteristics of, 29
  concepts of positive and negative, 50
  description of, 30, 31
  definition of, 69
  depletion, 87, 88, 89, ,91
  kinetic, 29
  high-wavelength, 32
  lack of, and herniated disk, 80,81

Energy (*continued*)
    losing, 69
    making productive use of, 32
    potential, 29
    upgrading your, 52
Enkidu, 71
Epic of Gilgamesh, 71
Extinction of species, 32

F
Fact collectors
    characteristics of, 89, 90
    E-cise menu for, 90, 91–97
    and human musculoskeletal
        system, 84, 85–86, 87
    and rigidity, 88
Fagles, Robert, 70
Fear
    Classic, 48, 49
    Lite, 48, 49
    and limitation, 43–52
    and neurotransmitters, 137
    and physical pain, 3, 47, 48, 49
Feeling, locating a, 44, 45
Feet
    proper movement of, exercise for,
        127
    and wrists, exercise for re-
        establishing linkage, 131
Flashlight tag, 23, 157
Foot circles E-cise, 105
Frog E-cise, 94

G
Gate keeper of body, 136, 137
Gene defects, 17
Glendower, 124
Glute muscles, E-cise for, 127
Golfer's grip, 95
Gravitational attraction, 32

H
Hamlet, 72
Hawkins, David R.
    and concepts of positive and
        negative energy, 50
    and glossary of positive and
        negative words, 52
    work on high wavelength energy, 19
Health
    awareness of, 38
    and mind-body connection, 8
Hearing as a traditional sense, 19
Henry IV, Part 1, 124
Herniated disks
    and Egoscue Method, 78, 79,
        80–81, 82
    favorite symptomatic treatments
        of, 80
High wavelength energy
    David R. Hawkins' work on, 19
    metabolic clips for ingesting and
        digesting, 58, 59
    and standing in an unbalanced
        position, 51
Hip crossover E-cise, 92
Hip lifts E-cise, 92
Hips
    repositioning and leveling, exercise
        for, 92
    rotation of, exercises for
        counteracting, 93, 96, 110, 129
Homer, 71
Hotspur, 124
Hubble, Edwin, and space matter, 30
Humankind
    and ability to change, iv
    and ability to deal with pain, v
    evolution as a community, 36
Human musculoskeletal system
    balance, 64
    design of, 56
    and distinctive posture, 5
    dysfunction, three categories, 76, 77

external interaction in, 55
and fact collectors, 84, 85–86, 87
feeling your way toward, 42
function and form of, 54
visualizing the role of, 26

I

Incoming stimulus, and click, 20
Increased mass, 25
Individual health, knowledge about,
    20, 21
Industrial Revolution, 41, 42
"Inert pharmacological compounds," 46
In-line gluteal contractions E-cise, 127

J

Joints
    load, exercise for proper
        positioning of, 109
    planar alignment of, 101

K

Kinetic energy, 29
Knee-pillow squeezes in static back
    E-cise, 91
Knees, full lateral movement of, 106

L

Law of gravitation, 37
Lipton, Bruce H. Lipton
    and gene defects, 17
    research on cells, 136, 137
"Living Force," 24

M

Mass, increased, 25, 26
*The Mathematical Principles of Natural
    Philosophy,* 37
Matter, description of, 31
Medical science
    and internal mechanisms of
        perception, v

Newtonian, 40
Memory, as repository of non-extant
    stimulus, 63
Mind
    aware, access to the, 121
    -body connection, 8, 11, 12
    as a brain process for recording
        and organizing experience,
        62, 63
Mitochondria, and destination of
    positive energy, 8, 9
Modern epidemics, 50
Mood swings, 3
Motivator extraordinaire, 49
Muscle(s)
    contracting-relaxing versus
        relaxing-contracting, 54
    functions of, 53, 54
    glute, E-cise for, 127
    hamstring, loosening, E-cise for,
        128
    skeletal, 53, 54
    working in pairs, 54, 55
Musculoskeletal system, human
    balance, 64, 66
    design of, 56
    and distinctive posture, 5
    dysfunction, three categories, 76,
        77
    external interaction in, 55
    and fact collectors, 84, 85–86, 87
    feeling your way toward, 42
    function and form of, 54
    misalignment, 58
    visualizing the role of, 26

N

Newton, Issac
    and clock metaphor, 37
    Law of gravitation, 37
    philosophy of, in medical science,
        37, 38, 39, 40
    philosophy of, overlap, 41, 42

Noble Eightfold Path of Buddhism, v
Nocebo effect, 123, 124

O

Objectivity Myth, 36, 37, 38, 39, 40
Odyssey, 71
Othello, 3
Outgoing response, and clack, 20

P

Pain
    chronic, as a symptom of energy
        deprivation, 19
    description of, 2
    as a generally recognized sense,
        20
    obsession with, 6
    and purpose, 47, 48–49. 50, 51
    questions about, 1, 2
    symptoms of, purpose of, 16
    symptoms of, suppressing, 4
Pain Free, 56
Pain-on/pain-off approach, 103
Particle energy, 31
Pelvis
    extension and stability of, exercise
        for, 111, 112
    positioning symmetrically, exercise
        for, 94
    proper tilt of, exercise for, 126
Perception, internal mechanisms
        of, v
Pessimists, E-cise menu for
    cats and dogs, 130
    downward dog, 131
    in-line gluteal contractions, 127
    standing forward bend, 128
    standing pigeon-toed at the wall,
        126
    static extension position, 129
    towel-roll settle with strap, 132
Physicians, perspective of, 39, 40

Placebo effect
    description of, 46, 47
    and pessimism, 123, 124
Plug and play, 26, 27, 28
Point flexes E-cise, 105
Posture
    balanced, 8, 65, 66
    change, and cells, 10
    as early-warning system, 18, 19
    good, returning to, 10, 11
    and mind-body connection, 8
    and musculoskeletal system pain,
        5
    poor, 10, 19
Postural therapy, 57
Potential energy, 29
Power vs. Force, 50
Prana, 36
Prefrontal cortex, and fallacy about
        longevity, 9
Premature aging and death, 33, 34–35,
        36

S

Sayings, 139–155
Senses, types of, 19
Sensitivity to temperature as a
        generally recognized sense, 20
Sensory receptors, 18
Shakespeare, William, 24, 72, 124
Sight as a traditional sense, 19
Singularity, 30
Sitting abductor press with strap
        E-cise, 112
Sitting femur rotations E-cise, 106
Sitting knee pillow squeezes E-cise,
        111
Skeletal muscles, 53, 54
Skeptics
    E-cise menu for, 105–113
    and musculoskeletal system,
        98–104
Speed of light, 38

Spine
 and hip, exercise for contracting
  and releasing, 107
 vertebrae, 77, 78
Standing arm circles E-cise
 for fact collectors, 94
 for skeptics, 113
Standing forward bend E-cise, 128
Standing pigeon-toed at the wall
  E-cise, 126
Standing quad stretch E-cise, 96
Standing at wall with pillow between
  knees E-cise, 109
Static back E-cise, 90, 91
Static extension position E-cise, 110,
  128
Storytellers, and musculoskeletal
  system imbalance, 71–75
Subtractive energy, 52
Subtractor energy, 52
Symptoms of pain, 16

T

"Taking things in stride," 70
Taste as a traditional sense, 19

"Them Bones," 25
Thoughtlessness, the virtue of, 13, 14
The Torah, and the age of the
  universe, 30
Touch as a traditional sense, 19
Towel-roll settle with strap E-cise,
  128

U

Universe, age of the, 30
Upper back
 exercise for releasing muscles,
  132
 exercises for strengthening
  muscles, 95, 113

V

Virtue of thoughtlessness, 13, 14

W

Wagner, Richard, 30

Y

You-mind, 21

Pain Free Living DVD Information

On this DVD, you will find a group of current and past Egoscue clients who have volunteered to tell you their stories and give you support. They were more than happy to participate because they were once where you are: searching for a solution.

You will also find detailed video descriptions on the DVD of each E-cise as the Egoscue therapists take you through each one.

DVD TRACK LISTING:

Personality Type
Suffering Is Optional
Testimonials
Energy
Helping A Friend
Egoscue E-cise Menus

Egoscue Contact Info:
Painfree@Egoscue.com or 1-(800)-995-8434

Music and lyrics by Caroline Jones

ABOUT THE AUTHORS

Pete Egoscue, an anatomical physiologist since 1978, operates the Egoscue Method Clinic in San Diego. His exercise therapy program is acclaimed worldwide for treating chronic musculoskeletal pain attributed to workplace and sports injuries, accidents, aging, and other conditions. He has been consulted by some of the biggest names in sports. He is the co-author with Roger Gittines of *Pain Free at Your PC* and *The Egoscue Method of Health Through Motion*.

Roger Gittines is a journalist and writer based in Washington, D.C.

About the Egoscue Method clinics:
Twenty-four Egoscue Method clinics operate in the U.S., Europe, and Asia. To learn more, visit the Egoscue Method website at: www.egoscue.com.